Beginner's Guide
to Applied Ecology

James Sholto Douglas

Beginner's Guide to Applied Ecology

PELHAM BOOKS

First published in Great Britain by
PELHAM BOOKS LTD
52 Bedford Square
London WC1B 3EF
1974

ISBN 0 7207 0777 3

Set and printed in Great Britain by
Tonbridge Printers Ltd, Peach Hall Works, Tonbridge, Kent
in Times ten on twelve point on paper supplied by
P. F. Bingham Ltd, and bound by James Burn
at Esher, Surrey

Felix, qui potuit rerum cognoscere causas.
(Happy he who has been able to learn the causes of things.)

Publius Vergilius Maro (Virgil),
70–19 B.C.

Contents

Illustrations

Acknowledgements

The author is indebted to the undernoted sources for permission to reproduce illustrations and wishes to record his thanks for their interest and support.

Photographs:
Chamber of Mines, Johannesburg, South Africa
Department of Forestry, Cyprus
Forestry Commission
International Synthetic Rubber Co. Ltd.
Nitrate Corporation of Chile
Press Association
U.S. Department of Agriculture
U.S. Naval Photographic Centre

Figures:
16, Science Journal
24, Baird & Tatlock Ltd.
25, Porteous Stills
26, Mr Graham Caine and the *Observer*
28, Mr John Wood
Other drawings are from original material prepared by the author.

Preface

Although there may be many excellent and instructive books available to the public on different aspects of general ecology it is difficult, if not impossible, to find any single work which provides a practical and easily understood guide to applied ecology for the average person. We hear much today of the need to conserve and improve the environment, but the dearth of accurate and useful information on how to set about doing this or how to regulate and adapt our daily lives in accordance with natural laws is very notable.

This book aims to give to readers in straightforward and simple terms an account of what ecology is, the principles upon which it is based and the purposes for which it can be employed. In addition, every effort has been made to include enough working guidance to show how we can all apply ecological methods in our own lives in order to solve not only many of our own problems, but perhaps also those of our neighbours and of the community at large. It is probably true to say that in some sense or other, everyone is trying to be an ecologist to the best of his or her ability. For do we not search our minds and hearts whenever a difficulty arises and seek for an answer that will bring about a satisfactory and harmonious outcome to the particular question at issue? If we are wise, we will also attempt to settle it, not by force or in a contentious way, but instead by remedial and befitting means so that it will not return later to worry or upset us. What we still lack, however, is access to the knowledge that science has accumulated and the practical guidance on how to utilise this in carrying out our purposes and achieving successful and happy results.

As life becomes more complex and the dangers to the world we know multiply, the foundations of existence sometimes seem to rock beneath us. By acquiring a sound and basic knowledge of

13

the structure and functions of nature, it is possible to see the reality underlying the course of events. Our natural surroundings are very important, but unless we can understand them fully we cannot hope to conserve and improve them. Once any environment is damaged or destroyed the task of restoring or reclaiming it may be extremely hard, even impossible.

In applied ecology, which means simply the practical use of ecological knowledge, to solve both daily and long-term problems, we have the means of improving and maintaining all that we love best in the world around us. Life, too, becomes far more interesting, and satisfying, indeed meaningful, when we can view affairs, so to speak, with an ecological eye. If you like doing or making things you will find applied ecology an infinitely rewarding and gratifying hobby or occupation.

Because we are a part of our environment – and this applies equally to the home, the neighbourhood, the country or the world, it is our duty to play our full role in conserving and bettering it. This book is, therefore, offered to the reader in the hope that it will provide not only interest and pleasure in perusing the contents, but also supply an agreeable introduction and guide to the science and practice of applied ecology.

J. SHOLTO DOUGLAS.

CHAPTER ONE

Looking at Life

Ecology may be defined in general and simple terms as the study of living organisms in relation to the environments in which they exist. In other words, what we have here is a science that seeks to probe and clarify the structure and the functions of nature, while at the same time investigating how men, plants and animals, as well as the groups which they form or the institutions which they develop, respond to their surroundings. The successes and the failures of individuals and societies are caused by many factors, including particularly modes of life, inherited or acquired characteristics, different patterns of thinking and outlook, and the habitats or sum totals of the conditions of the distinctive environments in which they are placed. All of these various aspects of existence demand serious and regulated studies designed to make them more intelligible to the ordinary person so that he or she may hope to find satisfactory solutions to numerous problems of modern living.

It is the purpose of ecology not only to provide the means of pursuing such enquiries in the most efficient and productive manner, but also to make available to anyone interested clear and profitable guidance, based on scientific principles, through the employment of applied ecological methods, to overcome daily or long-term practical difficulties and avoid disastrous mistakes caused by ignorance of natural laws. Thus, ecology is really looking at life, understanding it and building sure and safe pathways on which to go forward in harmonious relationship with our environment.

ECOLOGY'S PLACE IN SCIENCE

Ecology is one of the different basic divisions of biology, the general science of living things. The term ecology is derived from two Greek words: *oikos,* meaning house, and *logos,* signifying

15

discourse or speech. Literally, therefore, ecology implies a study of 'houses'. In fact, however, houses here refers to the much greater house in which we all live – that is to say the various environments making up the world around us. This world is the planet Earth, which supports and sustains us and gives us so many things, including the air we breathe, the ground we walk on or build upon, the food we eat, the water we drink and the raw materials for our industries.

Ecology, as such, is not an old science. On the contrary, it has only been formally in existence for just over one hundred years. The originator of modern ecology was Ernst Heinrich Haeckel (1834–1919), a German scientist and philosopher, who in 1865 became professor of zoology at the University of Jena. In 1869, Haeckel stated his view that individuals were the products of cooperation between the environments in which they lived and their inherited characteristics. He named this relationship 'oecology'. In course of time the spelling was simplified to ecology. Sometimes another expression is employed to describe this field of studies, that of environmental biology.

In 1859, Charles Robert Darwin (1809–1882) had published his work entitled *On the Origin of Species by Means of Natural Selection,* in which he set forth what was primarily an ecological theory of evolution, emphasising the importance of the environment as a selection agent over long periods of time. The activity and controversy aroused by Darwin's teachings largely overshadowed the work of Haeckel, so that Haeckelian oecology was more or less forgotten for a considerable number of years. However, towards the end of the nineteenth and the beginning of the twentieth centuries, interest in Haeckel's theories revived and the efforts of men such as F. A. Forel in Switzerland, E. B. Warming in Denmark, and E. A. Birge, H. C. Cowles and F. E. Clements in the United States helped greatly to expand and strengthen the science of ecology.

Despite the fact that ecology, as an organised subject, is of comparatively recent origin, it is important to remember that it was preceded by centuries of enquiry into natural history. Some of the material used today is even derived from the work of Aristotle (384–322 B.C.) carried out in ancient Greece. Twenty-two treatises of this philosopher, who was tutor to Alexander the Great, still survive. These writings include discourses on biology and meteorology. Aristotle considered that nature was always striving to perfect itself and he was the first person to classify organisms into species and families in order to show how they help forward this process. Plato, too, who lived in Athens from c.427–c.347 B.C., and was a follower of Socrates, made observations on the relationships between populations and the structure and stability of their institutions; while much later the medieval Arab scholar, Ibn Khaldun, contrasted the different modes of life practised by the inhabitants of rural and urban areas and communities.

During the first half of the twentieth century research workers in ecology tended to concentrate on the analyses of populations and communities. The scope of the science was widened greatly by the use of statistical and other methods and the interrelationships of ecology with subjects such as geography, physiology, biochemistry and the classification of organisms or taxonomy were stressed. Much attention was also paid to the study of climatic effects and the influence of the habitat or the conditions of the environment on living creatures. In addition, ecologists tended increasingly to evaluate the data they accumulated in their investigations in terms of conservation of resources and natural evolution.

These enquiries, though fundamental to the development of modern ecology, fell short to some extent, inasmuch as they emphasised mainly the descriptive aspects of scientific work. In other words, great stress was laid upon the recording of facts, the specification or delineation of conditions and relationships between organisms and the environments in which they lived and developed. This is, of course, pure science, which is content simply to discover nature's appearance as revealed in the behaviour of organisms and the circumstances prevailing at any given time. Virtually no attempt was made to translate the facts observed or the discoveries made into practical actions which could result in identifiable benefits for life on earth.

Fortunately, however, outlooks have changed during the past two decades. Most ecologists now place equal emphasis on studying how to utilise the functions of nature, instead of, as formerly, merely describing behaviour or conditions. This kind of approach views all organisms, both small and large, from the minute bacteria to the bigger mammals, as intimately linked functionally with plants in ecological systems according to well defined laws. The relationships extend also to climatic conditions, to the land, the towns and cities, to the rivers and seas and to all natural features. Thus it is the whole environment and its responses to change that figure prominently in ecological studies today. This shift in emphasis is what has made ecology such a dynamic science and one which is very deeply involved in the everyday life and progress of both individuals and communities in the modern world.

SCOPE AND PURPOSE

No living creature, whether man, animal or plant, can exist in complete isolation. Men and animals depend upon other organisms, especially plants, for their food supplies. Human

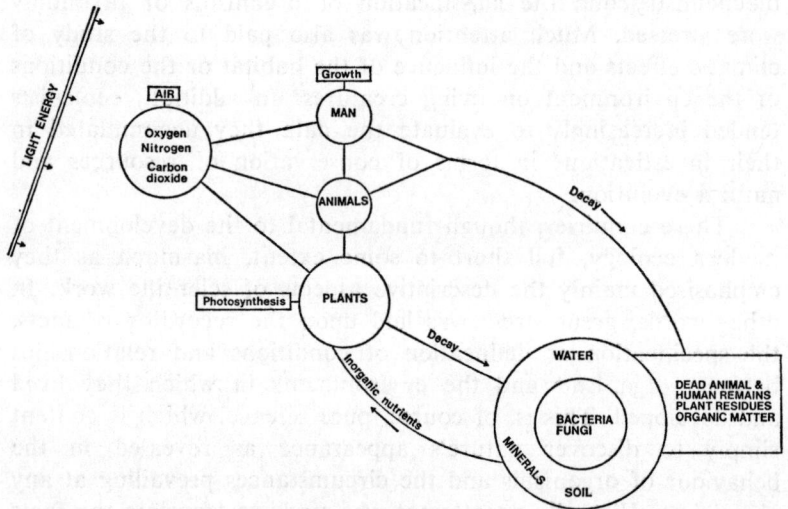

Figure 1   The interdependence of organisms and their food supplies.

beings need shelter and materials for clothing, while birds require nests in which to raise their offspring. Civilisation, as we know it in this century, is based upon continuous supplies of goods and efficient transportation, which are produced and maintained by utilising the natural resources of the Earth. Without green vegetation, life could not survive because both men and animals demand constant amounts of oxygen for respiration, which is provided by the ceaseless activity of plants.

In their turn, plants, although they manufacture their own food by means of photosynthesis, look to animals and human beings for some part of the carbon dioxide essential for this process. The supplies of mineral elements that they absorb from the ground are maintained by the actions of bacteria and fungi which break down the organic matter deposited in the soil by other organisms. Many plants depend on animals to disperse and carry their seeds to new areas and on bees and birds to pollinate them. It is also possible to see numerous cases of voluntary association between different kinds of creatures, either for protection, mutual benefits or other advantages. Common examples of this are men and dogs, the former providing food and shelter to the latter in return for guard duties, help in hunting and companionship; the crocodile and the crocodile-bird or plover, where the bird in exchange for security from predators picks irritating scraps of decaying meat from the crocodile's teeth and removes leeches from its throat; and the relationship between orchids and the microscopic fungus or mycorrhiza growing on their young roots, which takes the place of root hairs, absent in these plants, and performs the function of supplying moisture and food materials to the bigger species.

All communities, composed of different species, classes or grades of individuals, no matter how peaceful they might appear on the surface of things, are actually in a state of delicate balance. There is always intense competition going on between the various elements of which the groups are constituted for the basic necessities of life. Even plants, which cannot indulge in physical violence, as do men and animals, fight savagely for water and nutrients and especially for light. In vegetation, this struggle is waged by bringing about modifications in the material and chemical factors of the local environment. Larger plants strive to overtop and overshadow smaller ones and deprive them of vital illumination, without which they cannot manufacture their foodstuffs. In different manner, organisms possessing the power of locomotion, such as men, animals, birds and insects, fight for nourishment, territory and priority in sexual relations. Human beings seek mastery and control over valuable natural resources. Aggression is, in fact, a fundamental part of the life process and inherent in the competition that all organisms practise in order to survive and prosper.

To ecologists, the various reactions and behaviour of any animal or plant are just like the pieces of a jigsaw puzzle that must be put together in orderly form so as to present an accurate and complete picture of the subject. In explaining all the interrelationships existing between living creatures, their appurtenances and institutions and the changes that inevitably accompany their progress, ecology aims to build up a satisfactory understanding of the community as a whole. It is necessary to look at man as simply another piece in the grand jigsaw. The activities of human beings must be judged in terms of the effects that they produce on the communities of other species that inhabit the world and on the land from which food and raw materials are derived. This total view of the environment is fundamental to ecology, which always looks for integrated patterns of action and reaction in arriving at a proper understanding of any given situation.

One may well ask: what is the purpose of all this? Granted that we can study the behaviour of communities and the impact of different activities on the environment, so deducing factual information about the interrelationships and the life habits of organisms, but what can we do with the knowledge when we have acquired it? The answer is, of course, that we have to put this knowledge to practical use – to improve our own lives, those of our neighbours and indeed the collective lives of all the peoples of the world. There is still a vast gulf between many of the discoveries of pure science and their application in ordinary terms. This gap can only be bridged by the proper employment of applied science to reach down into the everyday existence of individuals and communities, thus placing within their grasp the means to surmount difficulties and improve conditions. It is the task of ecology, especially in its applied form, to supply both the knowledge, and the practical guidance on how to use it, so that we can all play our different parts in achieving more harmonious and satisfying lives and conserving and enhancing the environments around us. The great philosopher and physician, Albert Schweitzer (1875–1965), spoke much of what he called "reverence for life", and taught that existence should be based on respect of living things and the fullest development of resources for the benefit of all. By showing us the way to a proper understanding of the relations between living creatures and their environments, ecology offers a pathway to this goal. Moreover, it also provides the means, through its applied technology, for us to achieve this happy state.

DIVISIONS OF ECOLOGY

For the sake of convenience ecology is generally divided into a number of sub-divisions. This is done mainly for reasons of specialist studies and it does not alter the basic approach of the science, which is that of the conservation of natural resources and improvement of the quality of life. Nor does it affect the distinction that exists between pure ecology and applied ecology. While the former is concerned with the acquisition of fundamental information, the latter is devoted chiefly to putting into practice the knowledge obtained from ecological studies. The difference is in some sense artificial because many ecologists today are engaged actively in work that covers both these branches of environmental biology.

Important divisions of ecology include:

(a) *Terrestial ecology* is concerned mainly with types of environments and the interrelations between conditions on dry land.

(b) *Aqueous or aquatic ecology* may cover both the study of biological interrelations in fresh water areas, such as lakes and rivers or those existing in oceans and seas.

(c) *Animal ecology*. This section investigates the basic requirements of animals, such as their food, shelter, the habitats in which they live and how they reproduce themselves. Animal communities are studied and the ways in which these grow and change through time are determined. Another important concern is to define the climatic and other conditions that are most suitable for different animal species – in other words their distribution throughout the world. Animal ecology includes generally birds, reptiles, insects, various lower organisms, and fish, as well as mammals.

(d) *Plant ecology*. All types of plants are included under this heading, ranging from the bacteria and the fungi to the grasses, shrubs and trees, as well as those used in farming and gardening. The subject is vast because there are thousands of species of plants, very different one from another and they grow in many sorts of conditions. Thus, plant ecology is concerned with forests, deserts, prairies, tundra, and all forms of vegetation.

(e) *Human ecology* is the study of the structure and development of communities and societies of human beings. Apart from considering the processes by which mankind adapts to different environments, it must also take account of the technological systems and social organisations through which changes occur.

(f) *Population ecology*. Here we are dealing with the study of groups of organisms. A population may be defined as "a group of living individuals set in a frame that is limited and defined in respect of both time and space". When the reactions of organisms constituting a population are considered it is found that significant problems arise which are not always so evident in individuals or single units.

(g) *Urban ecology* is a comprehensive expression which is designed to apply to the peculiar environments of towns and cities and their suburbs. It is specially relevant today when so many people live in areas cut off from what we used to call natural surroundings.

(h) *Various*. In this category one may include other special sub-divisions of ecological study. Very often, ecologists concentrate on a particular aspect of the science, such as desert ecology, marine ecology, agricultural or horticultural ecology, which falls within or near to the general headings listed but contains certain features that distinguish it in notable details from the main subject. As new fields of study arise, we may look for further expansion of such investigations. It is, for example, very likely that an ecology of computers and machines may soon be a promising source of material for examination.

APPLIED ECOLOGY

Applied ecology is the subject of this book and consequently the preceding discussions of the objectives, history and purposes of general ecology are intended mainly to acquaint readers with the background and scope of the science. If somebody should ask me to provide him or her with a symbol that would create in simple and plain terms an image of the reality that ecology stands for, I would point to a fresh, newly-minted coin. Fresh, because this is a new and forward looking discipline; newly-minted since it is a young science; and a coin by reason of the fact that it has economic and practical values and as it passes from hand to hand emphasises the relationships existing between individuals, communities and the world they live in. Again, a coin has two sides with a different image on each one, just as ecology has two branches – pure ecology, which records facts and defines principles, and applied ecology which puts into practice the knowledge gained. Yet, at the same time, the coin is one entity, exactly as is the three-leaved shamrock which St Patrick used to explain the doctrine of the Trinity to the ancient Irish.

The word 'applied' is derived from the Latin *applicare,* to fold or fasten. By folding or fastening something we normally bring it to bear on something else so that it is put to use. Applied science means putting specific knowledge to use for definite purposes, other than its own end. The use chosen is normally utilitarian. Thus applied science is the opposite, when viewed in this context, of pure science, which does not generally proceed beyond the research stage. At that point, the applied aspects take over, after a period of development, and the discoveries are made to serve practical ends in the fields of technology or general consumption.

Of course, it is true that pure and applied ecology are interdependent and one follows naturally from the other. It would be a grave error to attempt to separate them, even if that were possible. But to use the information acquired by ecological research in the field of applied ecology requires human will and effort. Without these qualities, the knowledge accumulated would simply lie gathering dust in learned papers and scientific reports, unknown to the general public. Fortunately, in recent years, there has been a strong impetus developing amongst ecologists to put the results of their scientific work at the disposal of the ordinary person so that they can be employed in modern technology, industry, development, and conservation of resources, in order to make the lives of individuals and communities qualitatively and progressively better, and to ensure that the environment we all exist in is maintained and improved.

Only in the last twenty years has any realisation gradually come about that conservation of the world's natural resources is a matter of great urgency if this planet's rapidly growing population is to be adequately fed and provided with the raw materials that it requires now and in the future. Primitive human beings were few in number and lived in harmony with the other creatures and plants that surrounded them. The whole environment remained undisturbed and evolution or changes took place slowly in accordance with natural laws. But as man has accumulated technical skills and increased in numbers his influence has multiplied and in consequence the balance of nature has been very seriously upset in many areas of the world. In fact, in some places, what might be termed a rape of nature has occurred, with massive devastation of the environment. Formerly, nobody appeared to be aware of this spoliation of our inheritance and indeed it seems scarcely fair to blame entirely our ancestors, since they were ignorant of the dangers of what they were doing.

The same position cannot, however, apply today. For two decades, some ecologists have been warning ceaselessly of the foolishness and irresponsibility of this squandering and misuse of our natural resources. Modern man has therefore no excuse if he does not take stock now and begin to conserve, instead of to waste and destroy.

Applied ecology is the tool that science is offering to individuals and nations so that they can arrest their dangerous courses and turn to restoration and conservation while there is still perhaps time to do so. One might almost say that ecologists have come down out of their ivory towers and are mingling with the populace in order to place the knowledge accumulated at great effort and cost at the disposal of every man, woman and child so that it can be used in practical ways to make life happier and give back to harassed and weary populations the goal of a rehabilitated environment and harmony in their daily routine or surroundings.

The doctrine of unlimited growth, which incidentally is unknown in nature, so assiduously propagated in certain quarters today, is a complete misconception. Those who advocate this approach to modern problems are in reality scourging the environment and forging a vicious weapon that will eventually turn upon them and those they lead and destroy them all. The applied ecological approach, on the other hand, demands the use of methods at individual, family and community level which will provide a harmonious and integrated way of supplying the essentials of life, so that people can exist in contented and happy surroundings and look for meaningful objectives in life.

The use of technology in specialised fields is vital to civilisation. Conservation for example, demands skilled work in the spheres of agriculture, afforestation, drainage and engineering, as well as the construction of dams and the laying out of irrigation or land reclamation projects. The building of new houses, factories, suburbs and towns calls for contributions from architects, builders and other professionally trained persons or technicians. Economists advise on financial and trading matters, while governmental affairs are assigned to politicians and administrators. What has been so apparent is that narrow specialisation by different types of direction and control in most fields today has lead to very costly blunders which have stultified praiseworthy efforts for improvement. Indeed, it is often a case of blindness caused by excessive specialisation bringing about disastrous results. The root of all this trouble lies in the fact that an ecological approach was never even thought of or attempted. In contrast to the narrow views of specialisation, ecology looks at the whole environment and seeks to work out plans and practical guidelines which will take into account all the different aspects of a situation and the needs of every creature, institution, or resource that will be affected by developments so that a co-operative and harmonious prospect may be created. Ecology or environmental biology is the only science, and in its applied form the only technology, that can coordinate and integrate the varied activities and needs of different elements into one satisfactory and balanced whole.

Innumerable cases of loss and wasted effort have occurred when an ecological approach to problems has not been used. H. J. Oosting pointed out in 1956 that many of the dams built for water conservation became virtually un-serviceable after ten or fifteen years through silting up of the reservoirs. The fault did not lie in the construction of the dams, but in the failure to manage and control the use of the land in the catchment areas. Timber felling and overgrazing encouraged erosion of the soil, with the result that vast amounts of earth were washed down by rainfall and soon filled up the artificial lakes behind the dams. In one case, however, that of the Tennessee Valley Scheme, ecological advice was engaged and a proper ecological approach adopted, so that the beneficial effects of this great project on the environment have been long-lasting and satisfactory. The work undertaken in the Tennessee valley was necessitated by the gross mismanagement of the local land resources in the past. The aim, however, should be to anticipate and prevent destructive practices so that the land is kept from damage and maintained in good health. Prevention is better than cure. A. Leopold, writing in 1949, commented 'Practices we now call conservation are, to a large extent, local alleviations of biotic pain. They are necessary, but they must not be confused with cures. The art of land doctoring is being pursued with vigour, but the science of land health is yet to be born.' Fortunately, since that time, many institutions have established departments which are deeply concerned with the use of ecology in conservation and preservation or improvement of the environment.

Land health is vital to us all. A sick countryside means a sick nation, and this applies equally to sick towns, cities and suburbs, for the environment affects our ways of thinking, our physical and mental health, and our outlooks on life, as well as being the source of our food and other materials. Positive ecological policies of land health demand planned utilisation of land according to its productive capacities, and management that will ensure sustained, continuously profitable and maintained production. Productively does not refer only to food or raw material crops, but also to grazing areas, forests, or places set aside for nature reserves, centres of population or manufacturing, and other different purposes.

Farming and gardening are largely dependent upon the amount of solar energy that falls on the land. Given amounts of this energy are received by the land regularly according to latitude, extent of cloud in the skies and other factors. If there is no vegetation on the ground, the solar energy warms and dries the soil and is then re-radiated and lost as entropy for work purposes. Land productivity will depend on how the plant community existing in a locality can fix the solar energy in organic matter. The fixed energy passes from the plants to the animals or human beings that eat them, or through the animals feeding on the plants to the men, women and children who consume the flesh or other produce of those beasts, that is to say right up the food chain, until it is finally dispersed in respiration. Land can produce and support its animal communities, but the extent to which it can do so is limited by the quantities of energy that the

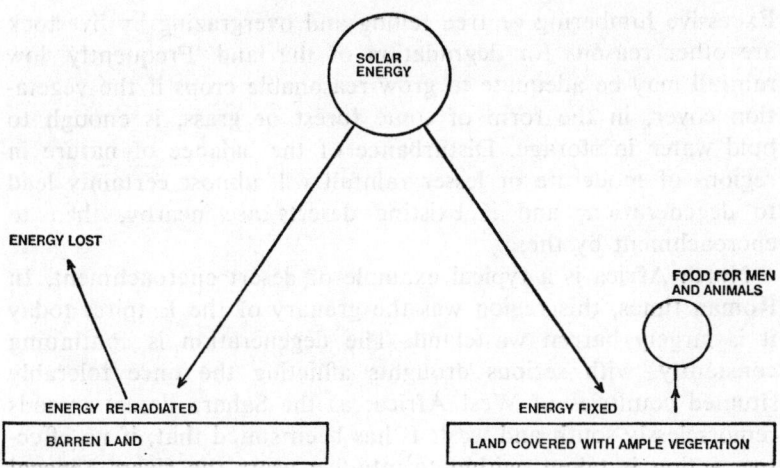

Figure 2 How vegetation makes land productive for man.

plants growing on it can fix in the first instance. Apart from climatic conditions which may be permanent, if man's activities do not alter them, the performance of vegetation in using solar energy is conditioned by the quality and quantity of the soil and water available. These are expendable assets and must be conserved very carefully to maintain productivity.

Soils are built up over thousands of years largely through the activities of plants and weathering of the land. Under natural conditions, a covering of vegetation clothes the ground and protects it from erosion. Thus, in Great Britain, the original native vegetation was mainly deciduous woodlands; in Scandinavia, it was coniferous forest, and on the American prairies or in central Asia it was grassland. These natural conditions, however, rarely fit in with civilised man's requirements and so he modifies them, causing an upset in the balance of nature. When this is done on a large scale or where the ill effects are uncontrolled and become cumulative, a decline in productivity of the land often occurs. The soil deteriorates or loses its ability to store water. Hence the great deserts and marginal areas of the world or the bleak and wind-swept moors and stark uplands. The basic cause is, of course, neglect of fundamental ecological principles. Often, wholesale erosion may occur, with the top soil blowing away.

Excessive lumbering or tree felling and overgrazing by livestock are other reasons for degradation of the land. Frequently, low rainfall may be adequate to grow reasonable crops if the vegetation cover, in the form of some forest or grass, is enough to hold water in storage. Disturbance of the balance of nature in regions of moderate or lesser rainfall will almost certainly lead to degeneration, and if existing deserts are nearby, then to encroachment by these.

North Africa is a typical example of desert encroachment. In Roman times, this region was the granary of the Empire; today it is largely barren wasteland. The degeneration is continuing constantly, with serious droughts afflicting the once tolerably situated countries of West Africa, as the Sahara desert spreads remorselessly south and west. It has been stated that, if no effective action is taken, within twenty-five years the rivers Senegal and Niger may disappear from the maps of Africa. In upland Britain, deterioration on a massive scale has taken place. The moorlands and highlands of northern England and Scotland were once covered with woods. The removal of trees has allowed valuable nutrients to leach out of the soil. The problem of restoring such marginal areas to productive use is essentially an ecological one and involves the establishment of pastures and forests integrated with their surroundings.

Industrial developments in many countries have led to a vastly increased demand for water supplies. It takes at least 3,000 gallons of water to produce one ton of steel; about 2,500 gallons to manufacture a motor car; and one gallon to make a pint of beer. The more water is consumed the less remains stored in the soil and consequently in different areas the water table has fallen considerably in recent years. To maintain water supplies for large cities and factories, it is essential to conserve and improve the catchment zones situated around the reservoirs that collect and store the water. Here, only a proper application of ecology will ensure that this is done efficiently.

The spread of insect pests and diseases in modern agricultural schemes is a source of considerable anxiety. Under natural conditions, such destructve organisms are normally kept in check by predators and there is less concentration of vulnerable or host plants and animals. Monoculture or the growing of pure stands of single species does away with variety and offers unrivalled chances for the outbreak of diseases and plagues. To counteract these epidemics, the farmer or gardener today has to resort frequently to massive doses of poisonous substances to kill off the attackers, with inevitable heavy expenses. The applied ecological solution to such problems is biological control. Sometimes this can be done simply by leaving intact neighbouring vegetation, perhaps hedges, which afford natural habitats for the pests; or at other times by utilising a number of measures, all of which originate in studies of environmental science.

Another example of serious damage caused by thoughtless exploitation of natural resources may be found in the Copperhill Basin area of East Tennessee. Fumes from smelters in the local copper mines were allowed to escape and killed off forest trees for many miles around. The district is now virtually a desert of raw and red gulleys where few plants can grow. This is only one instance of many similar cases. Mining has been responsible for extensive land degradation in places as far apart as South America, South Africa, Europe, and other regions, chiefly because no ecological advice was sought or considered in controlling the ill effects of the extractive operations on the environment.

Pollution is another serious problem facing individuals and communities today. This can take various forms, but the most notable are water pollution by industrial and domestic wastes; air pollution or smog; and pollution of the soil. Although the long-term biological effects of radioactive pollutants are a matter of some controversy, there can be little doubt that the manner in which such substances alter the environment and move in food chains are highly relevant to the welfare, health and future happiness of all living creatures. Ecology has much to say on these subjects and in the applied field few developments have been more important in recent years than the technique known as environmental engineering. Here, ecology and engineering are combined in order to deal with the constantly rising volume of man-made wastes.

One of the features of man's increasing activities on this planet has been a marked reduction in the number of species in existence. This lowering of natural diversity in the environment would appear to be a danger signal. It is considered, upon good evidence, that the more species present, the greater the possibilities for at least some of them to adapt successfully to changing conditions and the higher the opportunities for adjustment and survival. The introduction, without care and forethought, of new species into an environment can often result in the extinction of existing species. The best and most efficient communities are those that exhibit harmonious diversity. In planning agriculture, one should remember the great risk that may arise from excessive dependence on just a few species, of say, cereals or other crops, simply since the yields seem to be excellent and high at that point in time, because should a sudden epidemic of disease or a climatic change occur, all these specialised types could be wiped out almost overnight.

Exactly the same position applies to industrial development. Any product can lose its market or the source of raw materials from which it is made; they may become exhausted or too costly, or may even be cut off by different events, without much warning, thus reducing enterprises to ruin in a very short period. Consequently, ecology advises diversity and consideration of all factors involved before developments are begun – not only for today but for the long future ahead.

Ecology is involved greatly in the solution of many problems in the fields of public health and medicine. The control of the vectors or carriers of diseases, such as malarial mosquitoes, rats and rat fleas infected with plague bacteria, and ticks, lice, and mites responsible for spreading typhus or other illnesses may be effected by using knowledge obtained from study of the interrelations of vectors with their environments.

It is important to remember that in nature there are few 'good guys', and except for the notorious disease-producing agents or pathogens, not many 'bad guys'. Often, seemingly valueless organisms turn out to have beneficial and necessary functions to perform. Briefly, Nature – as the established order of things, is neutral on the whole. Mankind must start to think about the proper control and utilisation of nature, as well as general conservation and improvement, instead of going in for widespread extermination. This outlook should be directed towards the entire environment.

UNDERSTANDING NATURE

It will now be apparent to the reader that the purpose of ecological studies is twofold: to understand nature, by which we mean the whole environment – and this includes ourselves – and to apply the knowledge so gained to improve our conditions and manner of living. Once we have gained cognisance of the structure and interrelationships of individuals and communities, how they came into being and what factors maintain them in balance and equilibrium or cause them to decline, progress or change, as well as other essential details, we will be able to put this information to practical use in our daily tasks, to the benefit of ourselves, our neighbours and indeed the nation and the world at large.

On the applied side of ecology, studies of individuals, communities and their habits and institutions are closely linked with those of utilisation of resources, conservation and population increase. For centuries nature has been exploited with little thought for the future. The price for this is now being paid in terms of erosion, flooding, droughts, industrial pollution, the advance of deserts, shortages of raw materials, plagues of crop-destroying insects and fungi, starvation and malnutrition, over-crowding in one area while another is left barren and neglected, and countless other ills. All these problems are directly attributable to a shifting of equilibrium in the ecological balance of the world communities of organisms and the environment in which we exist. But in many cases, such difficulties could have been foreseen – and indeed were by many qualified persons – and prevented by the use of applied ecological methods, had there been better understanding of the dangers in the right quarters, so that proper remedial action was taken in time.

In the following chapters of this book we shall discuss in more detail the purposes of ecology, as well as the principles upon which it is based, and also how to use the science and technology in practice. Because the proper employment of environmental biology can bring about so many beneficial changes in our conditions, it is a subject of great importance today. Ecology, in fact, is a tool that all of us can use in our daily lives and work to guide us in making better decisions and in carrying out the routine duties that fall to our individual lots. In the past, perhaps, this science may have seemed a remote and involved discipline, far above the head of the average person, but today applied ecology is available to anyone who will take the trouble to read a little about it and utilise it thoughtfully and meaningfully in striving to solve the most difficult as well as the simplest of problems.

As the English poet Samuel Rogers (1763–1855), friend of Wordsworth, Scott and Byron wrote:

> "That very law which moulds a tear
> And bids it trickle from its source,
> That law preserves the earth a sphere
> And guides the planets in their course."

The law that forms the subject of these lines is none other than ecology.* Let us apply it in our lives and by understanding nature go forward in harmony and felicity with our environment to a better future.

---

*The word bionomics, derived from the Greek, *bios,* life, and *nomos,* law, is sometimes used as an alternative to the term ecology.

CHAPTER TWO

Organisation and Principles

In modern terms, the environment is not simply the place where a human being, animal or plant lives, but the whole range of factors that surround and play greater or lesser parts in influencing or moulding the organism's style of existence. It is, indeed, quite easy to see from common experience how much we are all affected by external changes and the movement of events or the passage of the seasons. Because the different components of any environment are constantly altering their relationships and time itself varies the quality and the quantity of life patterns, our world – and this means both our own individual small world and the much bigger world around us – is forever in a state of flux. In other words, natural environments are really unstable systems, of complex characters, with intricate relationships forming and evolving between their different constituents.

Each particular environment is actually unique in the sense that the transient or impermanent arrangements that keep it in being can never be exactly reproduced or duplicated again. There is, in fact, no natural limit to the progress of change, since though a system may become stable for a longer or shorter period, in due time it will inevitably start on a new path of movement. Nevertheless, the world environment, viewed as an essential whole, must always contain interdependent components and any division of these undertaken for study purposes is only arbitrary and convenient for investigators. It does not alter the oneness and completeness of nature.

UNITY OF THE ENVIRONMENT

The idea of the unity of the environment is basic to ecology. It has influenced all the aims and methods of ecological studies. Therefore, ecologists consider that the analytical practices of the physical sciences must be employed in environmental biology with great caution, because the removal of an organism from its natural surroundings destroys much of its integrity and affects its true responses. Similarly, if we take away any of the factors present in the natural environment in which a human being, animal or plant lives, the characteristics of the individual concerned – or indeed of a community or population – will be often unrecognisable and damaged. For example, it is possible to study the way in which an animal reacts to heat in a laboratory with precision, but the results obtained will bear little relation to the manner in which the same creature will tolerate temperature variations in its normal surroundings. This is because in nature, the heat changes also affect the animal's foes or its prey upon which it may depend for food, as well as its general living conditions. To sum up: analytical results may be accurate in the physiological sense, but as far as ecology is concerned they are grossly misleading in many cases.

INDIVIDUALS AND GROUPS

The interrelationships that exist between individual species and communities or groups and the environments in which they live are extremely complex. In order to simplify programmes of study, ecology divides in a convenient manner the investigation of individuals and populations. The detailed examination of the biology of individuals or individual species is known as *autecology,* a word derived from the Greek, *autos,* self, *oikos,* and *logos,* which means speech or discourse. The study of communities, natural assemblages of organisms or populations is, on the other hand, called *synecology,* which is also traceable to a Greek origin, being compounded from the terms *syn* or together, *oikos,* and *logos.*

At first, these two words may seem a little difficult, but use soon brings easy familiarity, and have we not absorbed and now use daily hundreds of more complicated technical terms in our everyday speech?

An ecologist making a study of the behaviour of individuals or an individual species of organisms will endeavour to accumulate information on how the subjects react to changes in climate; how they reproduce themselves and spread out; what their living conditions and circumstances are; what they eat and how they protect themselves; or the manner and style of existence that serves them best; as well as a hundred and one other things that may be noted about them, either singly or as a species. Autecology draws heavily upon some aspects of physiology, biology, genetics and other sciences, but always with the aim of providing as complete and integrated a picture as may be possible of the behaviour of organisms in their local surroundings.

Normally, synecological investigations should follow rather than precede autecological ones. This is because the key to real appreciation of the responses of groups and populations or communities lies basically in the characteristics of the individuals or individual species that make up the whole societies. It may be highly desirable to know first how the behaviour of single organisms affects that of their neighbours, as well as the way in which they respond to the differing conditions of life and the environments around them. Once equipped with a sound knowledge of the responses and habits of individuals, the ecologist will find it far easier to interpret the various relationships that he or she will observe in groups and communities.

LEVELS OF ORGANISATION

A convenient way of examining life is to look at what is called the concept of levels of organisation. This visualises a sort of biological spectrum or range of living patterns, running from the smallest entity to the largest one. The simplest form starts on the lowest level and the most complex stands at the top. The levels of organisation are as follows:

Protoplasm:	physical basis of life;
Cells:	unit masses of living matter;
Tissues:	aggregates of similar cells;
Organs:	parts fitted for carrying on a natural or vital operation;
Organ systems:	organs functioning together;
Organisms:	living creatures;
Populations:	assemblages of organisms;
Communities:	all populations of areas;
Ecosystems:	communities and non-living environments functioning together as ecological systems;
Biosphere:	inhabited land, water and air of the planet.

It is the last five levels, that is to say, organisms, populations, communities, ecosystems and the biosphere that are of major concern to applied and pure ecology. Organisms are of course, single units. Population is a rather variable term and is often used in slightly different senses, but it has here a wider sense than simply its original meaning of a group of individuals: it frequently implies groups of subjects made up of single species. The word community in its ecological context would generally include all the populations of any area. When we come to ecosystem, we are perhaps treading on unfamiliar ground for many readers. However, the term is simply a shortened version of ecological system. The ecological system or ecosystem means briefly the total of all the organisms in any place together with all the factors of the environment in question, considered as a whole. Finally, there is the biosphere. This refers to the portions of the world, ranging from as far beneath the land surface as any life may exist to the farthest reaches of the seas and skies where some form of existence might be possible to identify. Both ecosystem and biosphere are technical terms for nature, as we may know or think of it, but there are many ecosystems within the biosphere of varying type and characteristics.

Operating within ecosystems, and also on individual organisms or populations and communities, are many checks and balances, called technically *homeostatic mechanisms* or *homeostasis* (Greek, *homos,* same, and *stasis,* stoppage). These forces and counter-forces are, in a way, regulatory influences which prevent too violent changes. In animals, birds and men we are familiar with the controls that maintain internal body temperatures fairly constant despite fluctuations of warmth and cold in the surrounding conditions. On a larger scale, the carbon dioxide and oxygen content of the atmosphere that we breathe remains reasonably steady through the effects of natural activities in the biosphere. Nevertheless, homeostasis is subject to variation, often due to age, renewal, decay, or other factors.

Ecology always takes the broadest view possible of biological problems and in considering the spectra or levels of organisation we must regard as a continuous and integrated frontier line all investigations that we may make into the nature and functions of life and individual sections or activities. In order words, to understand any part we should also study the entire concept or pro-

cess, or we shall fail to grasp the real truth behind the phenomena.

ECOSYSTEMS

We have explained already what an ecosystem means in ecology
and it is now necessary to discuss such complexes in greater
detail. Ecosystems are the basic functional units with which ecologists have to deal, including as they do living organisms and
all the various factors of the environment, every part influencing
and affecting another and the whole supporting and maintaining
existence in different forms. An ecosystem can be looked at as
possessing two natural components: the self-nourishing section,
largely consisting of plants, which can fix light energy and manufacture foodstuffs from simple inorganic substances; and the other
or disparately-nourishing section, which utilises the materials produced by the self-nourishing part, rearranges them or moves
them, and brings about decomposition of more complicated
substances. This second section chiefly comprises man, animals,

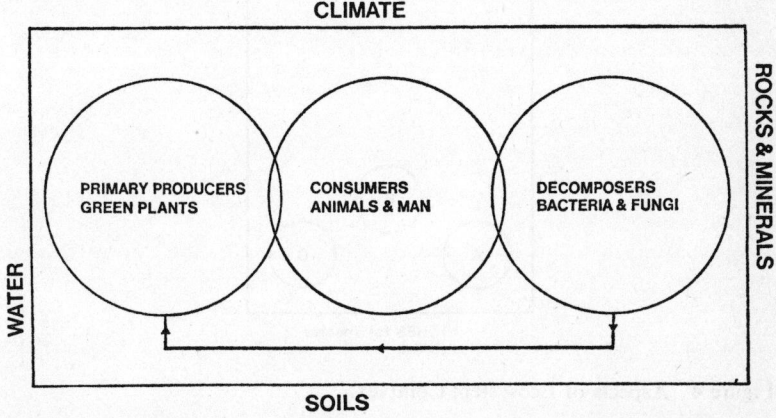

Figure 3 Diagrammatic representation of main components of an
ecosystem.

fish, insects, birds and different organisms and their numerous
activities. Structurally, the division must be carried further. The
basic elements of the environment, which are termed the abiotic
or non-living factors, such as the soils, the water, the rocks and
minerals, and the climatic conditions, exercise overwhelming

influence upon whatever forms of life may be present. The primary producers are, of course, the green plants; while the animals act in great part as consumers, eating other organisms and excreting much of the organic matter essential for continued fertility of the land, and finally, we have the decomposers, including the bacteria and the fungi, which break down dead material and release simple substances that can be used by the producers.

In studying ecosystems, it is often simpler to look at different aspects of the complex separately, without, of course, losing sight of their ultimate relationship to the whole. A good area to start investigations is with the *habitat* or the sum total of the conditions of the environment, excluding the organisms present. The habitat means the normal abode or locality in which an individual or population lives. Within different habitats, there will exist *niches* or recesses in which diverse individuals or species flourish.

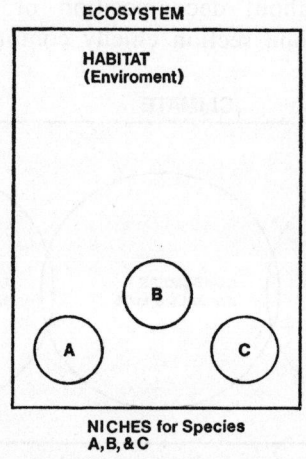

ECOSYSTEM

HABITAT (Enviroment)

B

A

C

NICHES for Species A, B, & C

Figure 4   Aspects of Ecosystem Complex.

A niche is very important. We can see in families how the various members have their own niches, according to their position or status and functions and the same principle applies to groups, communities and societies. In the case of man, the exact niche occupied depends much upon circumstances. Thus, in some areas, human beings are carnivores or meat-eaters; in others they may be vegetarians or herbivores; while in the majority of instances, they are omnivorous or mixed feeders. However, man's function in nature, together with his way of life, will depend a great deal upon the sources of food that are available. Different diets and standards of nutrition affect the habits and responses of human beings very substantially.

Ecological niches within given habitats may vary in type and quite often organisms may occupy contrasting niches in differing climatic regions. Apart from human beings' various food niches, we have also the case of coral reefs which rely on supplies of nourishment in markedly variable quantities according to the ability of the water surrounding them to provide them with either algae or zooplankton or perhaps both. In simple terms, one can refer to the habitat as an organism's address or habitation and the niches as more or less its job or profession. Niches differ in what may be called their breadth or living space. Some creatures can feed widely while others eat only certain parts of plants or are restricted to a very limited diet. Again, a number of organisms specialise in consuming, often as parasites, certain tissues or fluids in the bodies of other species. As might well be expected, the more specialised an organism is the more vulnerable it will be to change or upheaval. Non-specialised species can survive far more easily because their niches are much broader.

We have already noted that ecosystems contain both producers and consumers. The arrangements that exist between these two groups form a structure called the *trophic structure* (Greek, *trophe,* food). Within the trophic structure there may be several levels, where food exists. These trophic levels may be living materials or populations and are referred to as *standing crops.* Such crops may be either plants or animals, or perhaps in the case of some creatures, such as certain insects, hoarding animals, or man it may be stored or preserved food. The standing crop can be described in terms of the quantity or amount in any particular place, or as *biomass,* which means organism mass. We can measure biomass as living or dry weight, or in calories or by various other means. The standing crops are very important, since they not only represent potential energy or force, but also often act as buffers or safeguards against environmental changes or alterations in factors such as climate. Moreover, when they are made up of living materials or populations, they provide a space or habitat for these to exist in. For example, the trees growing in a forest provide fuel or food and give shelter to animals and men, in addition to ameliorating harsh weather conditions.

As well as the standing crops, there are also present non-living or abiotic materials, such as mineral elements. These include nitrogen, phosphorus, potash and other nutrients, coming under the category of inorganic chemicals. The amount of these elements in existence at any given time is referred to as the *standing state* or standing quantity. It is necessary to distinguish between

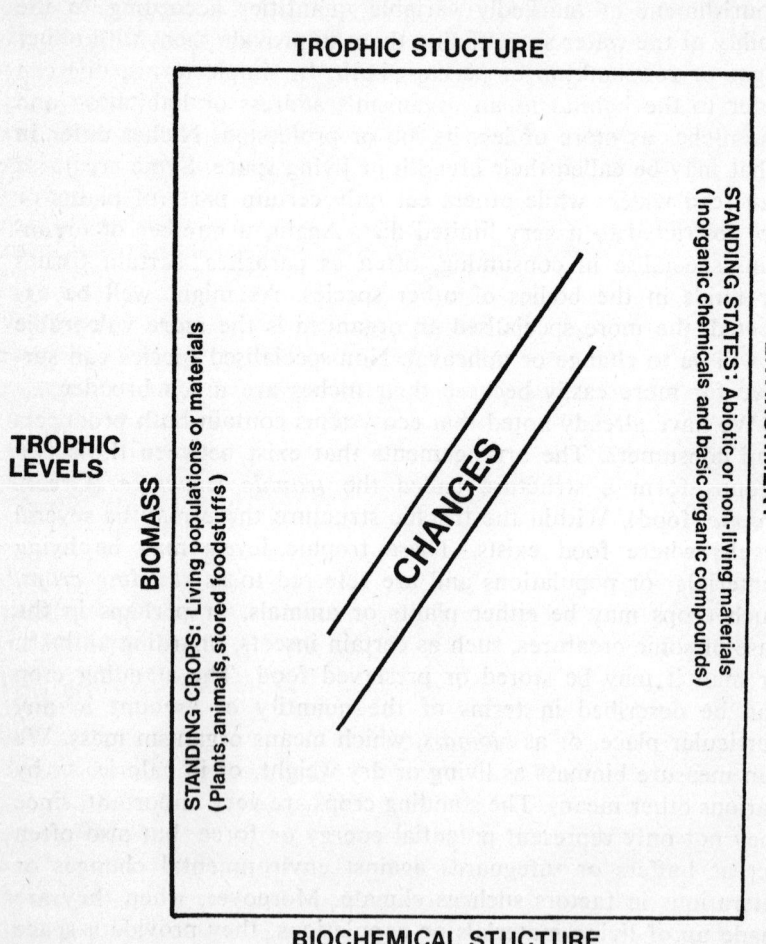

Figure 5 Scheme of trophic structure.

the amounts of materials and organisms present at any particular moment, or their average quantity over a period, and the rates of change in the standing crops and the standing states for each unit of time. To clarify this point, we may think of the total growing and stored crops in a farming area in any month or the figures for a year brought down to a general average; as compared to the periodic fluctuations that occur in the production, harvesting or consuming of food and stored stocks and the fertility of the soil maintained by fertilisers existing in it, which of course vary greatly.

It will be obvious that the quantities and distribution of the standing states, made up of inorganic chemicals, and of the standing crops, composed of living materials or populations, which are present either in the biomass or the environment, are extremely important factors in any ecosystem. In technical terms the whole amount of these substances or organisms and its arrangement is called the *biochemical structure*. We know that green plants contain chlorophyll, that is the colouring matter in the cells which is able to utilise the energy of the sun's rays to provide simple sugars and starch for food. The quantity of chlorophyll present in any given area of land is a subject of much interest. This substance is also frequently noticeable as greening on water surfaces, because the algae or minute plants or seaweeds floating in the water and serving as food for fish also contain it. Water, in addition, will be found to have dissolved organic matter in it, as well as mineral salts, unless it has been distilled.

We have seen how ecosystems may hold many species of organisms. The number and kinds of these species are very significant, being termed the *species structure*. Nature frequently encourages diversity and the relationships existing between different species and the numbers of individuals, as well as their distribution in communities, are of deep concern to ecologists.

Ecosystems can be thought of and studied in many sizes. For example, for the sake of convenience, one may wish to concentrate on such units as a lake, a pond, a plantation of trees and shrubs, or a particular piece of ground for certain investigations. Again, on a much smaller scale, one could study an aquarium, a greenhouse or conservatory, or a formicary or ants' nest. As far as human activities are concerned, the town, suburb or farming village are all good subjects for ecological enquiry. The impor-

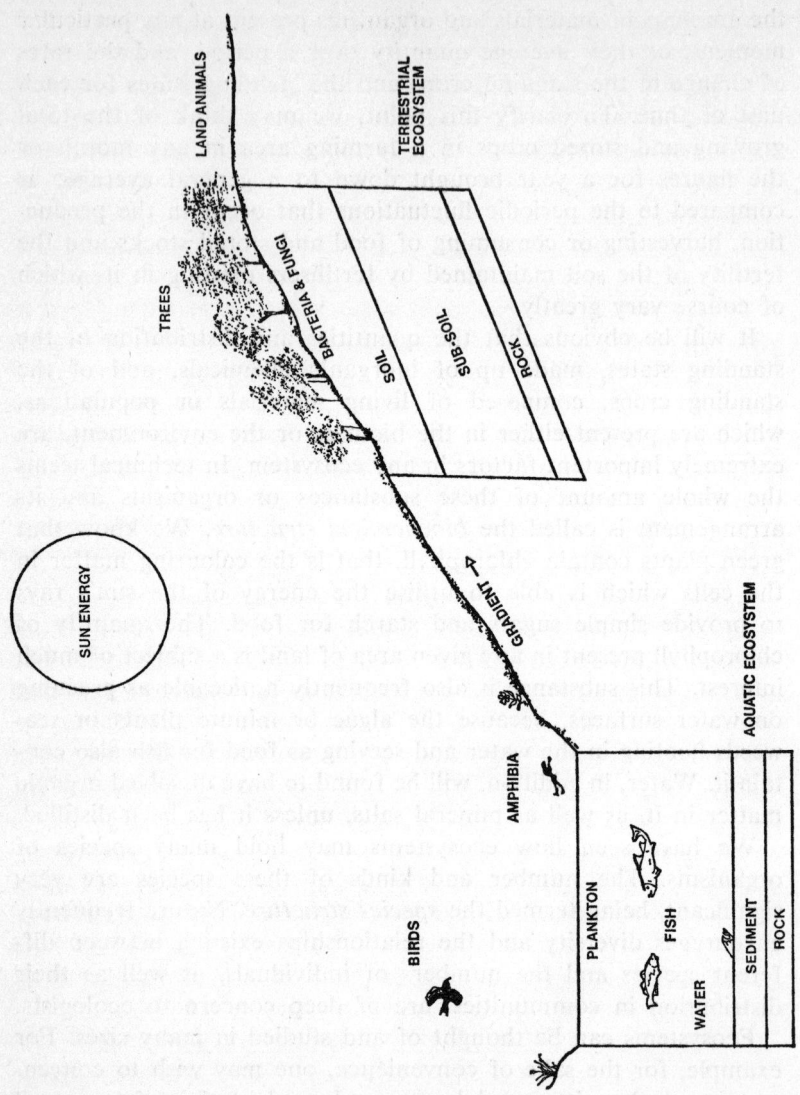

Figure 6   Arrangements in typical natural ecosystems.

tant point to bear in mind is that whatever unit you select as your ecosystem, it should contain major components of existence, which are operating together in some sort of stability, even for a short time, and functioning in a coherent manner. The biosphere really consists of a vast series of gradients integrated together to form one whole. Ecosystems are found in great numbers up and down these gradients. The larger and more diverse they are the more stable they will be. Just at which points, and where, we mark out the different individual ecosystems depends on experience to a great extent, for we may find evidence of units functioning satisfactory or less satisfactorily all around us. Well balanced ecosystems may last for very long periods, but ill-conceived ones will collapse or break down sooner or later. It is because so many of man's activities result in poorly devised ecosystems, fabricated to suit human purposes only, that these malfunctioning units, often termed civilisations, carry in themselves the seeds of their own destruction and will not last. As you progress in ecological knowledge, you will be able to distinguish between good and bad ecosystems and discover the errors and mistakes that modern man is making. It soon becomes possible to see which ways of life will last and bring happiness and which will not.

COMPETITION

Competition is a fact of nature, built in to the structure of our world environment and it is unlikely that its effects could ever be reduced in significant terms. Let us consider communities of plants. Intense competition takes place continuously between the different individuals and species growing in any given area for light, water, and food. Plants cannot wage violent struggles such as human beings and animals do, but they fight one another by indirect physical and chemical means. The method of operation is to alter the local environmental factors so as to eliminate competitors. Taller species overshadow smaller ones, depriving them of the illumination without which they cannot manufacture their essential foodstuffs.

Changes in the local climate, termed the *microclimate,* are often brought about by the dominance of bigger plants. These may reduce the capacity of lesser types to survive. Frequently, you can see weeds choking and destroying garden or field crops; in effect, pushing the weaker and more delicate species to the wall, so to speak, and eventually eliminating them. Sometimes, the process can be self-defeating, when big plants create a microclimate underneath them that prevents their own seedlings from growing to maturity. This means that in due course the species concerned will die out in that area and be replaced by other vegetation. So the nature of the local community will alter and new dominant plants will appear.

Violent competition arises between opposing groups of human beings, as well as between individual men and women, or even children, for the necessities or the luxuries of life. These may be presented by territory, sex, food, material goods of all kinds, or money. Animals, insects, birds, fish and other forms of life compete for living space, mates, and vital nourishment. When an ecosystem is in equilibrium, some sort of balance is secured and the different species and groups can exist in comparative harmony. Seen in human terms, nature is cruel because consumers eat producers and the producers in turn rely largely on the death of the consumers or their waste matter to obtain materials to aid further production.

Yet, in fact, nature is neutral. Human ideas of morality have no place in the evolution of the natural world, which is strictly utilitarian, subject to decay and revival, impermanent, and constantly changing. Competition is fundamental to this state of affairs, as the interplay between the factors of the habitat in which organisms exist and the inherited characteristics of the creatures or vegetation mould patterns of life. We do find that there is a large element of *chance* in nature. This is apparent in the process of colonisation. The dispersal of seed or the movement of men and animals frequently operate by hazard, with chance determining which individuals or species arrive at any place first. Fortuitous hybridisation may result in new types appearing, some of which may be successful, whilst others fail and are eliminated. Chance tends to decrease as time passes, since once communities develop, further progress is conditioned largely by the behaviour of the existing populations.

TOLERANCE

In ecology, tolerance means the ability to put up with the conditions of a habitat. If we consider an undeveloped area, we will see that some new arrivals can adapt to and thrive in the natural surroundings or modify them to their liking. Others will find the circumstances existing there unfavourable and will sooner or later die off. In other words, survival means the capacity to tolerate the conditions of the habitat. These will, in time, weed out weaklings and eliminate unsuitable types. However, in due course, the activities of the first colonists will alter the local habitat and so the balance of competition will be swayed in some manner or other. Consequently, further species or groups will enter the area and find that the changed conditions, produced by the earlier arrivals, are well within their tolerance. Once settled, such species may take control and perhaps force out or dominate the previous inhabitants. When a number of individuals or groups have colonised the locality there will emerge a definite structure in the whole community. We will then see each species occupying its own niche within the given habitat.

Tolerance is important in ecology, because it is necessary to know and understand the range and capacities of different species or populations, especially for applied work. Some individuals or species are specially adapted to tolerate harsh or extreme conditions, or will evolve to meet the circumstances imposed by the habitat into which they move. Adaptations can be physiological or through life processes or by means of structural changes in body and habits. These can arise from direct reaction to the new habitat, such as in the cases of plants which may alter their manner of growth, or through the production of genetically distinct forms of variable types selected by the harshness or rigours of the changed living conditions. In an opposite way, too favourable and easy a habitat will induce at times indolence and degeneration in the organisms dwelling in it.

AGGRESSION

To succeed in competition with other types, a species must be able to not only hold its ground but also to spread out and maintain its numbers. Plants do this chiefly by shading out their rivals, so depriving them of vital light. Human beings and animals accomplish the same ends by some form or other of violence. Whatever variation in detail there may be, however, the means employed all come under the designation of aggression. The process of aggression begins by the effective domination of the particular place where an individual or group lives. Once this has been achieved, the territory held must be enlarged. So the task of spreading out commences. Aggression or self-preservation is a deep-seated characteristic of all vigorous species and societies.

Viewed over the long term, it is undoubtably the most significant factor in the success of individuals and populations in their struggles for survival. Species which are not aggressive will sooner or later fail and be eliminated by nature. Indeed, whether we approve of this principle or not, we cannot alter it and ecology clearly shows that in real life aggression makes the biggest contribution of all to the success of any organism or society.

BASIC REQUIREMENTS

Let us now consider the basic needs of individuals and species in more detail. Organisms require food, shelter and living space in order to survive. These can also be considered as nourishment, recuperation and reproduction, the last noted impelling plants and animals towards expanding their territories, because without proper multiplication areas and room for progeny there would be no possibility of maintaining security.

Food

Living entities must obtain nourishment, according to the particular requirements of each type of organism, in order to survive. These foodstuffs have to be secured from the environment in which they exist and so food becomes a fundamental ecological factor. Generally speaking, the kinds of nourishment that make up the bulk of any species' diet are linked with specific adjustments to feeding habits. We can list the main feeding categories as follows:

(a) *Animals – Plant eaters or herbivores.* Many types of insects, such as aphids, feed upon plant sap or juices, possessing a tubular, sucking beak as an extension of their mouths; whilst others, including certain ant species, have thick crushing jaws that serve to crack seeds. Some species of lizards are vegetarian and these kinds have round and broad teeth. A long list of mammals, both domesticated and wild, are plant eaters, ranging from elephants to deer and giraffes and from horses and cows to rabbits and sheep. In these instances, the creatures have some grinding teeth.

(b) *Flesh eaters or carnivores.* Here we have two subdivisions, first the predators, which stalk their prey, kill by assault and then devour the victim; and secondly, the parasites, which feed on the flesh of their hosts continuously. Predators have usually

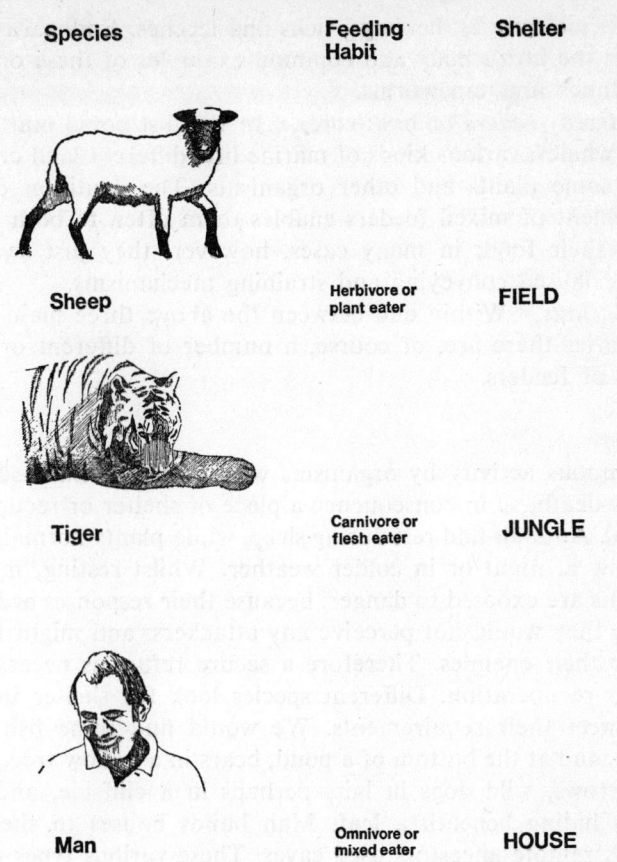

Species	Feeding Habit	Shelter
Sheep	Herbivore or plant eater	FIELD
Tiger	Carnivore or flesh eater	JUNGLE
Man	Omnivore or mixed eater	HOUSE

Figure 7 Examples of food and shelter needs of typical organisms.

some specialised equipment, varying in different cases, such as modified mouth parts, sharp claws, recurved teeth, or long protrusible tongues. The purposes of these parts are to overtake and hold the prey. A predatory organism first kills its victim, as a rule, before eating it. Parasites, on the other hand, do not desire the immediate death of their prey, but hope that it will live a reasonably long time, so that they may continue to feed upon it. Blood is much favoured as a diet by parasitic organisms. The saliva of parasites consuming blood generally possesses anticoagulating and anaesthetic properties. Blood feeders include fleas, most female mosquitoes, bedbugs, ticks and leeches. Endoparasites live within the host's body and common examples of these organisms are flukes and tapeworms.

(c) *Mixed feeders or omnivores.* In this list come man, whalebone whales, various kinds of marine life, different land creatures, even some plants and other organisms. The dentition or other equipment of mixed feeders enables them often to both cut and grind their food; in many cases, however, they just swallow it by specialised conveying and straining mechanisms.

(d) *Various.* Within and between the above three main feeding categories there are, of course, a number of different or graded kinds of feeders.

Shelter

Continuous activity by organisms would lead to exhaustion and finally death, so in consequence a place of shelter or recuperation is vital. Animals find rest during sleep, while plants normally cease to grow at night or in colder weather. Whilst resting, many organisms are exposed to danger, because their responses are slowed down, they would not perceive any attackers, and might fall victim to their enemies. Therefore a secure refuge is necessary for proper recuperation. Different species look for shelter in places that meet their requirements. We would find some fish buried in the mud at the bottom of a pond, bears in a hollow tree, rabbits in burrows, wild dogs in lairs perhaps in a cliffside, and caterpillars hiding beneath a leaf. Man builds houses to shelter in, but his remote ancestors used caves. These various types of shelter or homes are niches within a habitat.

We have already discussed habitats and we can now proceed to classify the main type to be found in different areas. It is convenient to group them as follows:

(a) *Aqueous.* (i) Marine or salt water, including polar, temperate and tropical regions. Under this heading come rocky, muddy and sandy shores; the surface waters of seas; and the deep or abyssal oceans.

(ii) Salty or brackish waters, such as estuaries.

(iii) Salt lakes, such as the Dead Sea, the Great Salt Lake and Lake Eyasi.

(iv) Fresh water, comprising standing waters in marshes, bogs, ponds and lakes. The last noted may be polar, temperate or tro-

Pollution and degradation in British cities: a slum housing area in the
north of England

Left: Pollution and overcrowding: cars queuing and blocking the Kingston by-pass in the south of England. *Below:* Marine and shore pollution: oil from the wrecked *Torry Canyon* tanker in Porthleven harbour, Cornwall

Above: Gulley erosion in Tennessee, U.S.A. Caused by bad farming and land use. *Below:* Wind erosion. A dust storm in the United States. Soil is blown off land damaged by bad husbandry

ECOSYSTEMS

Left: Deciduous woodland. Beech trees with seedling regeneration. *Above:* A tropical forest in south Senegal. Note thick, luxuriant undergrowth. *Below:* A natural coniferous forest, Oregon, U.S.A.

pical and include shorelines, middle depths or surfaces, and deep waters or lake bottoms.

(v) Flowing waters. These cover cold and hot water springs, chemical springs, all types of streams and rivers, some of which have rapids and falls and quiet pools, and even quite tiny brooks.

(b) *Terrestial.* (i) Aboveground, which includes flood plains, of various types of land; hills and mountains; grasslands, of tall and short grass species; forests, of deciduous or evergreen types in temperate and tropical zones; deserts, of sandy or rocky kinds; and tundra or other regions.

(ii) Underground, such as caves and deep caverns.

(c) *Parasitic.* These may be ectoparasitic (external to the host's body) or endoparasitic (internal).

(d) *Various.* Composite habitats such as the nests of ants and bees, the lodges of beavers, or the towns, cities and suburbs of mankind. Certain organisms are also found in the atmosphere.

The above noted categories are not hard and fixed. There are many graduations in habitats, depending on differences of climate and location and there may be numerous habitats within one ecosystem. Environmental influences alter conditions and exercise both short- and long-term effects. Sometimes, habitats are used continuously by the same organisms; at other periods they may be occupied by temporary residents. Here we may note the cases of migratory birds. In winter, certain creatures, such as bears hibernate. In summer, heat and drought may make the habitat unsuitable. Of interest are nocturnal animals which can utilise an area at night, alternating with diurnal animals which are active there by day. Various organisms pass different stages of their lives in contrasting habitats, such as fresh-water clams, May and dragon flies and salmon. Other species can range over many series of habitats because they will tolerate considerable environmental variations. This ability to survive in differing circumstances is termed *vagility.* A typical example of vagility is found in the puma, which thrives equally at sea level or in mountainous regions, or in man, whose habitats cover the five continents.

Organisms are constantly adjusting to their environments, as well as through their activities exercising modifying influences upon local conditions. Natural selection over long periods of

time produces populations which are better adapted t
circumstances than perhaps their ancestors were.

Living space

The question of living space or territory is really pa
reproductive process. Reproduction means the multipli
the species and necessarily demands more territory fo
sion. It is a basic drive of all organisms. Weather affect
activities and the laying of eggs or the pollination o
Reproduction also depends a great deal on adequate fuod and
shelter, freedom from attacks by predators and parasites, low
incidences of diseases, general cooperation and other influences.
Failure to reproduce means the decline and ultimate death of
populations. Excessive fecundity can, however, result in overcrowding and shortage of foodstuffs, if further territory is not
available.

COMMUNITIES

Ecology shows us that no organisms can exist in complete isolation. Plant eaters must be associated with the vegetation upon
which they depend for sustenance, while carnivores and parasites
have to live within reach of their prey or hosts. From these facts
has been developed the principle of community. Communities
are natural gatherings of populations of species linked together
with other species in groups or assemblages. Sometimes, ecologists call a community a *biocoenosis* (Greek, *bios*, life, and *koinos,*
common). Biocoenoses are made up of different populations and
can be of various sizes, compositions or degrees of complexity.
There is a distinction between the nonliving environment or physical conditions and the community, which is the living environment or biocoenosis, but both are combined to form the ecosystem,
which we have already discussed. We know that each species has
certain inherited characteristics which permit it to exist in given
environmental circumstances and so it follows that all the various
populations in any area must be able to live tolerably in the
locality in question. All environments are complex in nature and
are composed of physical influences or factors, such as heat and
cold, sunlight, rain, soils, water supplies, and other significant
effects; as well as biological factors, including sources of foodstuffs, shelter, pressures of population, predatory and aggressive

activities, diseases, and many more connected attributes, which may bring about change or modify life patterns.

Major communities are those which are more or less self-sustaining and possess the power to regulate themselves. In other words, they are at the survival stage. Provided they receive adequate radiant energy from sunlight, such assemblages should continue at a level that ensures longevity. Good examples of major communities are forests, lakes, oceans, prairies or grasslands and similar kinds of biocoenoses. Some common basic features may be noted in major communities, such as stratification or a structural level of society; exchange and reuse or recombination of food materials; and a common habits of periodicity, or timing of activities.

Minor communities are not normally self-sustaining. These smaller groupings are susceptible to decay, often experience rapid changes, and cannot be considered viable or permanent, being frequently of temporary or transient nature. Examples of minor assemblages would be mounds or casual deposits of animal dung, heaps of compost, rotting branches and trunks on the forest floor, pond bottoms, or even a coral reef.

To consider the main features of major communities in a little more detail, let us look more closely at structural levels, use of food and timing.

Stratification

The populations of species are regarded as being arranged in a vertical series of horizontal layers, called *strata,* as well as in a series of concentric layers having a common centre, termed *zones,* from the outside or periphery to the middle of the community. There are thus both horizontal and concentric layers in all major assemblages. Each grouping will be in contact with others at its boundaries, so marginal territories exist where the different communities meet. These areas are called intergraded sectors or in technical language, *ecotones.* So we have, for instance, a seashore standing between the ocean and the land, or a suburb lying between city and countryside. Ecotones are not major communities, because they are not self-sustaining and are only kept in being by the presence and intergrading of the major communities around them.

In forests, we can see stratification clearly, reaching up from the underground or root area through the forest floor, the herbacious cover, the shrubs and smaller trees, to the larger species and the eventual canopy of the woodland. Within the different strata, there are numerous microclimates, forms of animal life and peculiarities. These give rise to various adjustments and there is a common pattern of organisation for particular strata in widely separated forests in contrasting regions of the world. Dissimilar species may occupy a given stratum in two forests, fulfilling parallel roles, but having related needs. This interesting phenomenon is called the principle of *ecological equivalence*. It is not difficult to see this law operating in many spheres or styles of life. Societies of human beings have their various ranks and classes, with persons of different attributes performing comparable tasks, though the groupings or assemblages may be distant one from another in space or time. It is an interesting exercise to work out what or who are the ecological equivalents today of the slaves of Greek or Roman times or relate the structural levels and strata of contrasting civilisations and political societies throughout the world. Man is not, of course, the only highly organised species on the Earth, and profitable studies – perhaps yielding useful lessons for us, can be made of ants, bees, and termites, in this connection.

Exchange and reuse of food
These processes, which include interchange and recombination of nutritional materials, are known collectively as community metabolism. Metabolism is the sum total of chemical changes in living matter. The first phase of *community metabolism* is the formation of foodstuffs, termed the anabolic or building up section. The opposite of this is the catabolic or breaking down phase. We have, so to speak, two industries at work in anabolism: the microbiological industry, covering the breaking down and reduction of organic matter, chiefly dead plants and animals, by bacteria, into inorganic salts, which are utilised by the higher or green plants and algae for part of their essential food; and the photosynthetic industry, responsible for the production of plant carbohydrates, which are manufactured in the photosynthetic process by green vegetation and some bacteria, and when combined with the inorganic salts absorbed by these plants, form plant protein. The last named is made avail-

able as plant tissues for the community to feed upon. Catabolism, on the other hand, is carried out mainly by man, animals and fungi. Herbivores eat the plants and are in their turn consumed by predators, parasites and hyperparasites. So we can see that all organisms are in some way dependent upon the microbiological and photosynthetic industries, which rely upon each other to function efficiently in the food cycle of the community.

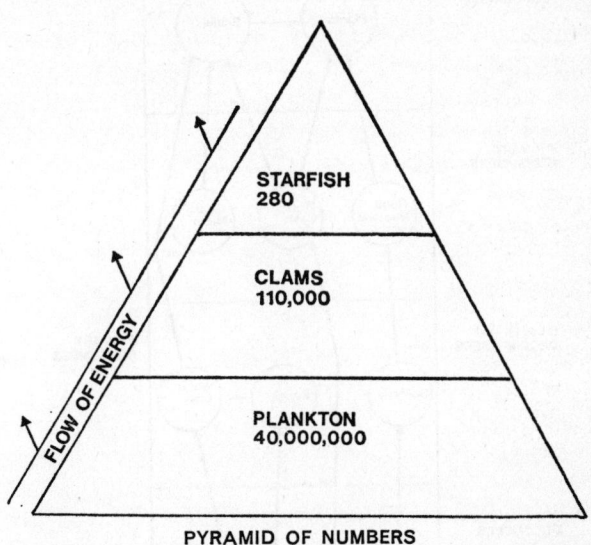

PYRAMID OF NUMBERS

Figure 8 DIAGRAM OF A PYRAMID OF NUMBERS. Note the much larger number at the base, where the organisms are small, compared to the comparatively sparse total of the main predator.

The circulation of foodstuffs in a community is called the food web. Food chains are built up in various areas or groupings and can be followed by observation of the life patterns in the environments in question. Species may, however, eat different foods in different places or in various regions of their geographical distribution, as well as in the succeeding stages of their life histories or during the seasons of the year.

In food webs, it is found that the numbers of small organisms

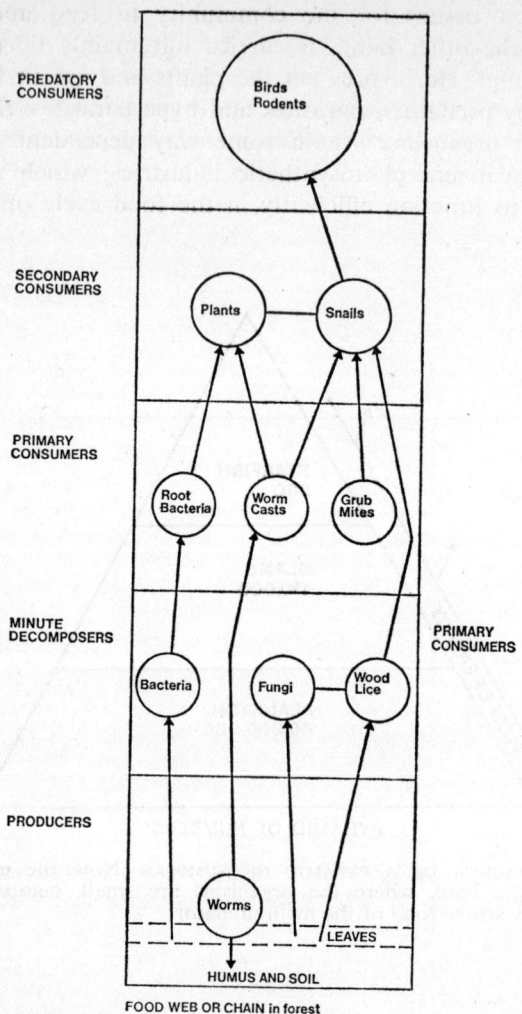

FOOD WEB OR CHAIN in forest

Figure 9 Food Web or Chain in forest.

in any given area will exceed the numbers of larger ones. It is possible to construct a diagram called a *pyramid of numbers* to illustrate this and also to show the relationship of size to abundance. Small creatures have greater fertility rates than bigger organisms. Now, the energy value of the food eaten has to balance eventually the effort expended in catching and assimilating this nourishment, so predators usually devour animals inferior in some way to themselves, but generally in the next lowest size level. This tendency, it will be noted, is not a fixed one, inasmuch as characteristics other than size may form the criteria. Thus, a leopard may attack and kill a horse, a pack of wild dogs hunt and catch large deer, or a man shoot an elephant. In all cases, however, the effort will be minimised, by devices such as surprise, strength of numbers, or in the case of human beings by employing weapons.

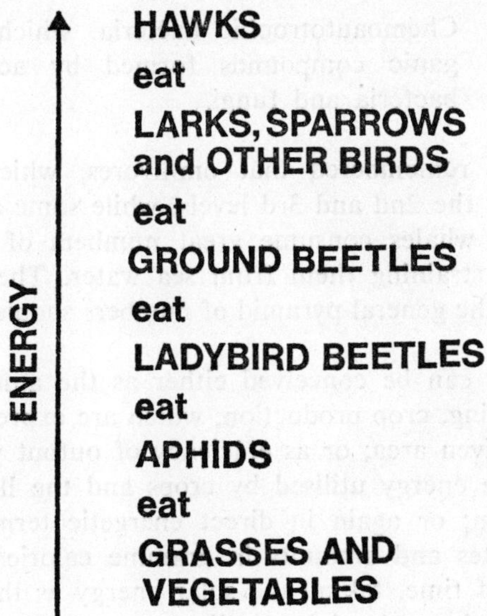

HAWKS

eat

LARKS, SPARROWS and OTHER BIRDS

eat

GROUND BEETLES

eat

LADYBIRD BEETLES

eat

APHIDS

eat

GRASSES AND VEGETABLES

ENERGY ↑

Figure 10   Working of a Food Chain.

We have already mentioned trophic levels and biomass in ecosystems. A community pyramid of numbers may have several trophic levels or levels of feeding interrelations. Each level can contain a varying number of species and there may be different quantities of individuals within each population of species. A simple illustration will clarify this arrangement:

Trophic level	Occupants
1st	Photosynthetic plants or photoautotrophic bacteria. Producers manufacturing carbohydrates.
2nd	Herbivores, or primary consumers, eating green plants.
3rd	Carnivores, or secondary consumers, feeding on herbivores and others.
4th	Bacteria and fungi, nourished by dead plants, herbivores and carnivores.
5th	Chemoautotrophic bacteria, which simplify organic compounds formed by actions of the bacteria and fungi.

It must be remembered that omnivores, which are mixed feeders, eat at the 2nd and 3rd levels, while some animals, such as whalebone whales consume great numbers of very minute organisms by straining them from sea water. These and other exceptions to the general pyramid of numbers should not be overlooked.

Productivity can be conceived either as the annual, together with the standing, crop production, which are expressed in terms of yield per given area; or as efficiency of output viewed in the context of the energy utilised by crops and the livestock feeding upon them; or again in direct energetic terms, reckoning production rates and amounts in gramme calories per unit of area to unit of time, taking the solar energy as the total available. In general, productivity declines as the place of the producer in the pyramid of numbers becomes higher. Thus the output of edible fish, expressed in yield per area of ocean, is far lower than that of the zooplankton upon which the fish feed. In other words, at every trophic level, when one organism eats another, only a very small portion of the energy stored up in the tissues of the victim actually becomes available to the consumer. The rest is lost as heat in the environment.

Ecology is much concerned with the problems of productivity. There is, in the world, an enormous surplus of solar energy that is not used by plants and animals. In addition, human beings demand ever-increasing food supplies, but return very little available energy to the cycle of nourishment. In course of time, mankind may not find that global food stocks or crops can support greater population numbers; and moreover, the conservation of natural resources will be affected adversely, unless ecological guidance and practices are employed to rectify the position.

Periodicity

The timing of the activities of organisms in their searches for food, shelter and living space or reproduction may be grouped into the categories of periodic and aperiodic or non-rhythmic responses. Most important community activities are periodic and are related to influences such as day and night, temperatures and rainfall. The physical environment imposes different procedures upon group actions, which are often necessary for health and survival.

In major communities, we can see three general kinds of periodic activity:

(a) *Seasonal.* These include plant growing seasons, animals' mating periods, hibernation and aestivation (dormancy in the dry season), relations between leafing, flowering and fruiting of many plants with day and night lengths during the year, and migration of species. In technical terms the study of periodic and seasonal events is called *phenology.* A sequence of phenological changes, related to environmental factors, and followed over a yearly cycle is termed seasonal succession or *aspection.* It is possible to divide the year into a series of periods connected with weather movements or the condition of food supplies which will coincide with the peaks of abundance of different populations, characteristic behaviour of various species or structural changes. Two examples of such phenomena would be the rutting season of deer and the appearance of butterflies from chrysalises, which were originally formed by caterpillars and remained dormant during winter.

(b) *Lunar.* In some animals, reproduction is correlated with lunar or tidal events. Typical cases of those of palolo worms and other species which swarm and spawn at definite periods during certain months of the year.

(c) *Diurnal.* This word refers to day and nocturnal or night activities. The twilight periods may also be significant and are called the auroral or dawn and the vesperal or dusk, or collectively the crepuscular, events. Green plants manufacture carbohydrates during daylight hours and distribute much of it by night throughout their tissues. Many small animals which inhabit the upper layers of the sea move to the surface area during night-time and downward during the day. In communities, there is generally a quite well defined night life and also an equally obvious phase of day activity. Nocturnal creatures possess special adjustments to their eyes which enable them to utilise all available light during the darker hours. This is very noticeable in cats, flying squirrels, and many snakes. Common fireflies have luminescent organs which glow at night. Similarly, other animals which live in areas of brilliant illumination may have adapted eye lenses which reduce light intensity and glare. Most communities can be divided into diurnal and nocturnal groups or organisms, a fact which increases the number of niches in the habitat and makes the assemblage in question more complex.

Aperiodic activities do not show a rhythmic relationship with the usual cycle of day and night. On the contrary, populations and individuals may be sometimes active and sometimes inactive or some specimens will be moving about whilst others are resting. This is a feature of animals living in underground areas or inside decaying tree trunks in forests. Such environments are fairly stable and not affected by light or darkness. Many kinds of ants and termites follow aperiodic patterns, as well as to a lesser extent bees and wasps. Man is also aperiodic, and the more civilised he becomes the farther away he moves from rhythmic habits of living.

SUCCESSION

Ecological succession is the growth and change of communities through time, as distinct from group organisation. We can divide succession into two sections: first, the physiographic or naturally descriptive component, influenced by geography and the physical features of the environment; and secondly, the biotic or living component, which is determined by the organisms making up the community itself.

Physiographic influences follow a successional pattern and include erosion of the soil and its movement by wind and water to new areas, weathering of rocks and changes in the topography of regions. Vegetation plays a very important part in these developments. Biotic effects are caused by the actions of plants and animals within communities. Organisms deposit waste material, they die and decay and trample or disturb the land or perhaps overgraze and damage vegetation. Often, one or more species may be displaced by new populations, which then colonise and take over the local habitat. The process of community change is induced and regulated by the combined actions of physical and living influences acting upon the environment and the groups present in it.

Community changes will proceed until a stable situation is attained. In the early stages, we have what is termed a pioneer community, but eventually this will become a climax community. In between there may be many sequences of development. A whole series is called in ecology a *sere*. The final result will be a climatic climax in which, given the local circumstances, the physical and biotic changes are more or less stabilised and are tolerated by the organisms and populations present. Such a climax would normally persist unless affected by new factors, including violent changes, as for example, earthquakes, tidal waves, damage by man or other calamitous events. It is, of course, a fact that succession may be interrupted, modified or stopped within any sequence. Human disturbance is a common cause of such checks or alterations, resulting in the creation of an artificial community known as a disclimax. Undisturbed succession and development result in a number of natural sequences called primary seres, while where man controls or indirectly influences the processes, the sequences become secondary seres.

Very often, purely local conditions play a deciding part in succession and development instead of the overall and prevailing climatic influences. Thus, the soil or edaphic factor may limit the ability of plants to thrive in an otherwise suitable place. Aqueous sequences, such as swiftly flowing water and standing water, can modify considerably the circumstances existing in different areas. The same rule also holds good for local rainfall.

Within the whole community, many smaller sequences may occur. These are called microsequences or microseres and describe what happens in dung heaps, rotting piles of wood or fallen trees, in ant nests, in individual houses or dwelling places and similar

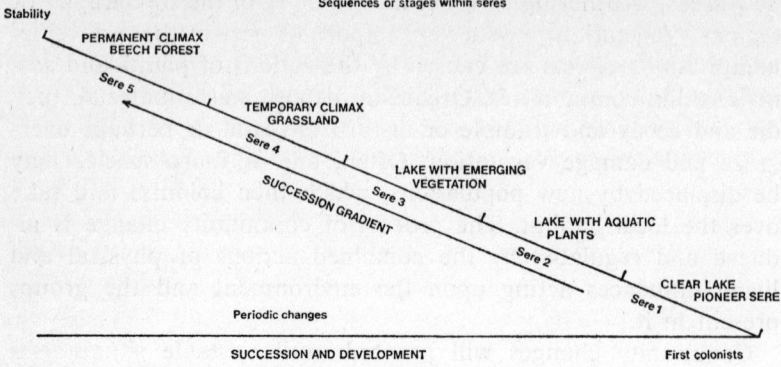

Figure 11   Succession and Development.

situations. All such successions do not actually reach a definite climax stage, but are incorporated into the major community as it develops and matures.

CONVERGENCE

When a community matures there emerges what is called the principle of convergence. This lays down that there is a general tendency for all seres to progress, decay or fulfill themselves and eventually meet in a common development. It is through convergence that local and particular movements become identified in the end with the overall pattern of a region and produce a comprehensive and integrated climax. Convergence has many broad implications and explains not only how communities incline towards certain general life styles and outlooks, but also why various features and conditions emerge in specific situations.

BIOMES

A biome is the largest ecological unit. The word is derived from the Greek *bios,* life, and *metron* measure. Communities of all kinds are distributed widely throughout the world and are influenced by climatic, edaphic and aquatic factors, as well as topography. There are many communities within a biome, which is seldom continuous, but covers a large area and consists of a single climax type, with variations in composition and subsidiary seres. In course of time, the effects of convergence will influence all biomes.

The terrestrial biomes cover about 30 per cent of the world's surface, with those designated marine or composed of oceans and seas accounting for the other 70 per cent of the globe. The major biomes on land may be listed as: equatorial forest, temperate grassland, tropical grassland, desert or semi-desert, temperate deciduous forest, coniferous forest and tundra or snow and ice desert.

Water biomes are all really parts of one immense biome, which contains many communities. The ocean and sea biome is actually a single and self-sustaining major assemblage, having numerous internal groupings. Marine organisms are usually divided into the categories of plankton or drifting organisms; nekton or animals (fish) that move against currents; and benthos or forms that inhabit the ocean floor and other subaqueous places, such as crabs and sponges. The layers of the seas are divided into vertical and horizontal sectors. The pelagic division is the bulk of the water mass and contains an euphotic or lighted zone and an aphotic or unlighted zone. Normally, the upper two hundred and fifty yards of water are illuminated to greater or lesser extent. Plankton live here as well as most nekton. The benthic or sea floor division can be demarcated into littoral and deep-sea systems. Within these sectors there are several sub-divisions, ranging from high tide levels on the shore through the continental shelves to the middle areas and then right down into the abyssal zones, where water pressure is intense.

THE GENERAL PICTURE

This necessarily brief account of the organisation and principles of ecology should now have given the reader a good general picture of how environmental biology functions and what its basic precepts amount to. Before approaching any kind of study or investigation it is essential to know the rules and methods by which you are going to operate. Otherwise, a chaotic situation would arise and the results secured would be of very little use in planning practical activities or bettering conditions. Nature not only abhors a vacuum, but also dislikes haphazard and confused procedures. Though the element of chance may play a certain role in life, once the fortuitous event or events have actually occurred then the sequences will follow quite well-established patterns, within the general context and direction of the ecological principles that we have discussed in this chapter.

To utilise applied ecology efficiently and beneficially in our lives does not, of course, require that we should all have a very detailed and intimate knowledge of the complete organisation and principles of the science, but it will help us greatly if we are at least familiar with the general outlines. This enables us, when we see a certain condition or situation existing to recognise which ecological principles are being worked out in the particular circumstances, and thus to know what may be the final climax and whether the ultimate results may be success or failure. It will also assist us to discover dangers in current life styles, to ascertain if different actions or behaviour are good or bad, and to mitigate or overcome difficulties by recourse to the laws and practices of ecology.

A student or practitioner of applied ecology should be able to organise his or her life through putting into daily use the knowledge and methods learned from simple memorising of the basic principles of the science, just as we keep in our minds, say, the rules of civilised behaviour and etiquette or the ability to do straightforward mathematics or spell and write our language. Though ecology may be a new subject to many persons, yet it is fundamentally nothing more than general good sense and the application of observed and natural rules, discovered by diligent investigations into the functioning of the world around us, to the betterment and harmonisation of the lives of individuals and communities and, indeed, of the entire biosphere or that part of our planet, including the air, land and oceans, upon which existence as we know it depends for survival.

CHAPTER THREE

The Spoilt Earth

In terms of human history the Earth is very old. Long before the
first primitive men fought with mammoths and sabre-teethed
tigers for the right to survive in what must have seemed to them
to be a harsh and relentless environment, our planet had passed
through innumerable changes extending over very many millions of years. From the beginnings of life to fishes and reptiles
and from dinosaurs to early mammals stretched long eras. Continents arose and were submerged in the oceans, vast forests
flourished and decayed and glaciers ground and pulverised the
surface of the land. Man was, indeed, a latecomer to the world
scene.

During all those countless centuries of pre-history nature
maintained a balance or equilibrium, despite the numerous
changes and successive alterations in the forms of life existing
on earth. We might say that nature was in command and that
natural laws, which we now have defined for us in the science
of ecology, directed and held together the development and progress of the planet. Life, of course, existed only in the biosphere,
that small fraction of the world, extending to about seven miles
below the level of the seas and some five or slightly more miles
above the surface of the land, which contains the water, soil and
air vital to organisms. Within these limits, and with constant
adaptation to the many convulsive and epoch-making events
that shook the globe, evolution slowly progressed, until finally
man, as we know him today, appeared.

MAN AND NATURE
When the numbers of human beings existing in communities on
the earth became greater, men started to interfere with nature.
At first, this may have been necessary to a certain extent because
food had to be grown, houses and settlements had to be built

and dangerous animals had to be repelled. However, as the populations increased forests were burned, hilly lands were devastated by cutting down trees established there which led to extensive erosion and loss of soil, as well as climatic changes, and wars between different groups caused widespread destruction. In course of time, man discovered how to make more elaborate tools and finally machines. This last step ushered in the industrial revolution of the nineteenth century. Man's competence then seemed to be at its highest and greatest level and the future of the human race appeared to be virtually unlimited in its prospects. Moreover, better medical knowledge and improved sanitation conquered many of the diseases that had threatened health and welfare. Consequently, a very notable rise in population occurred, so that today the number of people alive in the world totals about 3,680,000,000 and this may reach double that figure by A.D. 2000. Because of his vast power and technical competence, modern man has come to dominate the Earth, often displacing nature and seeking to use all its resources for his own gain and profit.

Unfortunately, in the process of aggrandising themselves human beings have frequently ignored natural laws, and often without any thought for the future, have caused very serious damage to the environments in which we all live. Indeed, it is no exaggeration to say that during the past one hundred years more injury has been done to the biosphere than in all the preceding centuries put together.

The signs of this spoliation, with accompanying deterioration, are all around us and may be seen clearly even to the untrained eye. Thus modern man has raped nature and brought serious evil into the world. Urgent measures are necessary to restore balance and repair the damage done, before it is too late. Ecology is the tool that we can each of us use to restore our planet to its proper equilibrium, and this is why it is so important for all interested persons to know just where, how and why the Earth has been spoilt, in order to be able to apply ecological methods in the best and most efficacious ways, to put right the wrongs done. A spoilt Earth means the degeneration and eventual death of the whole human race with much misery and suffering arising during the process.

*　　*　　*

LIFE AND DEATH

Viewed in natural terms, life is part of a continuing operation – the movement of the world through time – in which individuals constitute only fractional portions. The process of global development has existed for millions of years and may well persist for many aeons. Primitive men and our historical ancestors thought of birth and death as fairly commonplace events, just as animals do, forming natural links in the chain of life. Modern man, however, is conditioned to look upon death and everything connected or associated with it as extremely distasteful. Even scavengers and carrion-eaters, such as vultures, are regarded with horror and often persecuted, although they are designated specially by nature to clean up dead or putrefying and decomposing matter which might spread diseases if left around. But just as birth is essential, if life is to continue, so death is a necessity if room is to be found in the world for new generations. It is reliably estimated that since the year 600,000 B.C. to the present day some 77,000,000,000 persons have been born on Earth. Without the normal incidence of death where indeed would all these people find space to live or produce their food on this planet?

We must, therefore, recognise the fact that sad though it may be, death is essential to life, and existence, as we know it, could not continue if no person ever died. This fact applies equally to men, animals and plants. Future generations expect that they will have a place to live and move in, bequeathed to them by our ancestors and ourselves. If the place is kept in good condition, our descendants will praise and remember us gratefully, but if they come to inherit a bad and deteriorated world they will execrate us and our folly.

Modern man, especially in North America and Europe, attempts to prolong his natural life. This is not wrong in itself, particularly if achieved by the elimination of diseases, but when he accompanies this aim by crowding populations into slums, poisoning the air, water and soil on which they depend for existence, and creating serious erosion and pollution, then the only eventual results will be famine and a breakdown of civilisation.

Despite the exaggerated pronouncements of some self-styled authorities, there is no question of over-population in the world today, nor likely to be for generations. What there is, however,

C

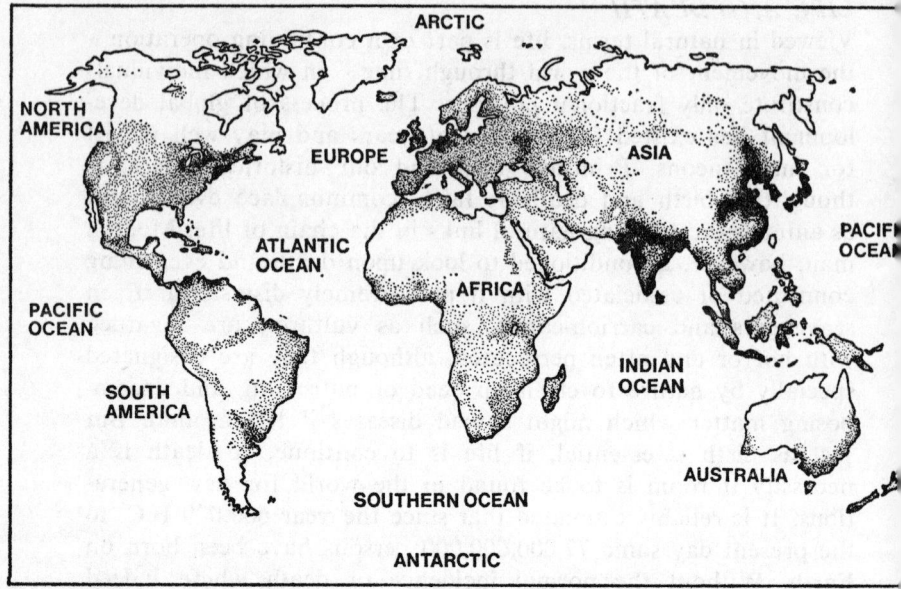

Figure 12 HOW HUMAN POPULATIONS ARE DISTRIBUTED THROUGHOUT THE WORLD. Note the very marked overcrowding in certain sectors, whilst other regions are sparsely peopled or virtually uninhabited. Thickly populated areas are shown in black and those not favoured for settlement by man in white.

is very serious overcrowding of people in certain areas, while other localities are neglected, uninhabited and lying idle. Science possesses the knowledge and technical ability to feed and care for a world population of as much as 50,000,000,000 persons. What are lacking are the will and support to put this knowledge into practice. This is not to say, of course, that we could ever have had any hope of feeding and accommodating all those people who have been born and died since 600,000 years before the birth of Christ, as well as the present and any future inhabitants of this world, but it does show the capacity that is now available to us, provided that a proper distribution of human beings throughout the globe could be arranged and full use made of modern methods of food production.

WASTE OF RESOURCES
The overcrowding of human populations and the marked increase

in the number of people living in certain areas of the world have led to much wastage of natural resources. Both minerals and fuels are being used up today at an extravagant and alarming rate. In addition, the programmes of excessive industrialisation and continuous growth which are being pursued by most governments are causing pollution on a vast scale. Much more is being taken out of the earth than is being put back into it in terms of materials and effort. In due course, this will bring about the collapse of the biosphere surrounding the planet and render normal life impossible. In other words, the present conduct of industrialised man is making unacceptable demands on the natural world.

Whether intended or not, man's actions in destroying forests, for example, affect wildlife. The habitats of many animals are eliminated when woodlands are cleared, and it is frequently impossible for the dispossessed creatures to find new homes. Consequently, they soon die or are killed. Numerous plants are also uprooted or perish. A large number of different animals and plants have become extinct as a result of persecution or annihilation by man. All of these species formed parts of nature's plan for the world and often played very useful roles or performed beneficial functions in their local areas. Today many more animals, birds, insects and fishes are threatened with total elimination by the activities of human beings. The hunting and killing of tigers and jaguars, chiefly for the sale of their skins for making women's fur coats, at high prices, has reduced the populations of these animals to a very low level. There are now only a few thousand tigers left in India, where once these proud beasts roamed the jungles in considerable numbers. Similarly, the elephants and lions of Africa constitute at the present time merely a poor remnant of the formerly vast herds and prides that ranged over the territories of that continent. Yet these kinds of life, and many others, all contributed towards the balance of nature on earth and were meant to share with man in the benefits of existence on this planet.

Human beings are great discoverers, but unfortunately they seldom know how to use what they find or invent in proper ways. Man's colonisation and settlement of the world has given rise to destruction and pollution of the environment. Vast wastelands have been created, while the bulk of the population is pressed and herded into squalid and noisome cities, which are then held up by many as the climax of civilisation. These pockets of settlement are grossly overcrowded and are the direct cause and origin of several serious problems that face mankind today. The physical effects of such overcrowding are numerous and range from starvation and nervous debility to crime, suicide and cruelty. The air in modern cities is polluted by fumes and in many towns there may be slow poisoning of the inhabitants by traces of lead and mercury present in water and food supplies.

This technological age may have produced in some ways an easier type of life, but it has created many worries for individuals and societies, particularly over questions of regular employment, the need to keep constantly acquiring more goods and possessions, and the incidence of mental illness. People flood into cities to seek work far faster than it is possible to provide houses and accommodation for them. Consequently, millions of the inhabitants of urban areas live in dwellings that are really not fit for habitation and in grossly overcrowded conditions. Local overpopulation in towns causes different stresses and strains and makes individuals hard, self-seeking and aggressive, since they are compelled to strive for standards of living, money and goods which they are persistently told they need and which are in limited supply. The final result is always a waste of human resources, because few can give of their best in such unsatisfactory circumstances.

There is a serious danger in doing things without any proper form of control and without thinking about the long-term effects that actions or practices may have upon organisms and the environment. A typical instance of this lack of care and forethought was the discovery of the insecticide DDT. The value of this chemical, as well as its efficacy, is undoubtedly very great, especially in malarious areas, but unfortunately it may often be more harmful than beneficial to general conditions. Similar criticisms also apply to systemic insecticides, which are taken up by the roots of plants and absorbed into the sap stream so that any organisms which suck up such sap will be poisoned even after a lapse of several weeks from the time of original application of the chemical. BHC, Aldrin and Dieldrin are other toxic pesticides which kill many organisms rapidly. The organo-phosphorus compounds, including HETP, TEPP, Parathion, and Fluoracetamide, based on another compound, are powerful mammalian poisons.

All these chemicals can kill useful animals, birds and insects and man himself. Consequently, despite their advantages for some farmers, they are more dangerous than they are valuable, and have been banned in a number of countries because of their poisonous and polluting natures. Much damage has been caused by employing such toxic substances in agricultural and domestic work, with immense loss of resources both in life and materials.

Poisonous wastes are continually poured into rivers and lakes or into the seas, while foul and toxic effluents from factories and other premises pollute and degrade water supplies and the land as well. The testing of atomic and nuclear bombs and devices has created explosions which upset all forms of life for hundreds or even thousands of miles away from the experimental areas. Bigger and faster jet aircraft damage the world's cloud cover and exercise potentially adverse effects upon the global climate. Here again, in all these, as well as many more, cases, grave damage is being done to the biosphere, with waste of vital materials.

CONSERVATION

Because every new technical advance poses so many more problems for us all it is essential that no effort should be spared to preserve and conserve our environment. Conservation does not just mean guarding the world's wildlife or stopping a little soil erosion. On the contrary, although it includes these important tasks within its purview, it also covers a much broader field – that of the care and maintenance of our planet considered as one whole unit. Protection of the Earth's natural resources, which means all that exists under the planet's surface, on the five continents or in the five oceans, or in the air around us, is a vital and fundamental duty. We depend on the soil for much of our daily food and this too needs caring for, fertilising and safeguarding from damage by bad husbandry. We should cease from releasing poisonous substances into the environment and stop destroying the land or turning it into desert and barren waste. Other forms of life than our own deserve due consideration and have the right to exist, so we must recognise the significance of the roles played by animals, birds, insects and fishes on the land or in the sea.

Conservation, in short, means survival. Cessation of destruction and replenishment of nearly exhausted stocks are imperative if our own species is not to inherit a silent and unthrifty world. After all, our planet is unique in our solar system – we should have to travel many millions of light-years far away to another galaxy to even have the possibility to find another quite like it. Though it may be that in the future man will succeed in colonising our neighbouring planets, Earth will still remain as the essential base for human activities. If we squander and dissipate our world's resources then the ultimate fate of mankind will indeed be grim and calamitous.

A DOOMED PLANET

In this day and age, Earth is a dying planet. It is slowly succumbing to the exactions and ravages of man and unless the process is checked and reversed before it is too late, the final result will inevitably be the total pollution and disorganisation of our world with great loss of life. This unhappy outlook is not based on exaggerated or scaremongering predictions but upon observed facts. The position has been for some time the cause of increasing concern and mounting alarm amongst ecologists and workers responsible for the development and extension of other applied biological sciences. It is feared that unless nations, governments and individuals awaken soon to the gravity of the situation serious disasters of unprecedented magnitude will undoubtably overtake the human race before many decades have passed.

Certain important points stand out. The first is the high level of present-day world population and its rapid rate of growth; secondly, the supplies of basic foodstuffs are apparently insufficient and inadequate to meet demand; and thirdly, there is the inability of the comparatively small existing areas of good and fertile agricultural land to produce the vast quantities of extra nutriment that will be required to support a substantially larger number of inhabitants on this planet in the future. Consequently, it has been predicted by certain authorities that food shortages of calamitous proportions will arise in the Far East by the year

2000 and throughout the world by 2030. Indeed, these forecasts may err on the side of caution, and it is not unlikely that whole-sale starvation may come in some places even before the turn of this century. At the present time, between three and five hundred million persons suffer locally from actual lack of food, and up to one-half of the Earth's people experience a greater or lesser degree of hunger, combined with shortage of vital proteins and chronic malnutrition in various forms.

These facts are enough to dispel any attitude of complacency. Moreover, policies of birth control and limitation of population offer no panacea or solution. Birth control, as sponsored by the western nations, is regarded generally by underdeveloped peoples merely as a device cunningly thought up by the rich countries to prevent the poorer territories from increasing their populations and so strengthening their power.

Now, as we have already mentioned earlier, science possesses the knowledge and ability to raise food production by safe and intensive methods to a high enough level to feed adequately a world population some twelve or more times greater than it is today. Not only would special systems of crop cultivation be employed to supplement the output of the fertile farms and gardens but the vast barren deserts and wasted lands that cover so much of the Earth's surface and are at present virtually unused and unpopulated, could be brought into fruitful bearing by the proper employment of modern ecological technology. Such pro-grammes would renovate, preserve and conserve natural resources and arrest the decline in our environment.

At this point, perhaps the reader may say 'All very well, but when world population does eventually reach the 50,000,000,000 mark, can you still go on raising food production, and if not, what will happen then?' The answer to this question must be that we cannot be sure yet whether science may make further advances during the next century or two in the field of crop growth or food manufacture that will enable even more people than the stated figure given above to be cared for, but that it could reasonably be expected that one of three things will happen: either large num-bers of human beings will have emigrated to new colonies estab-lished on the other planets of our solar system, or future changes of living patterns and standards will have favoured voluntary forms of further population limitation or else mankind in its

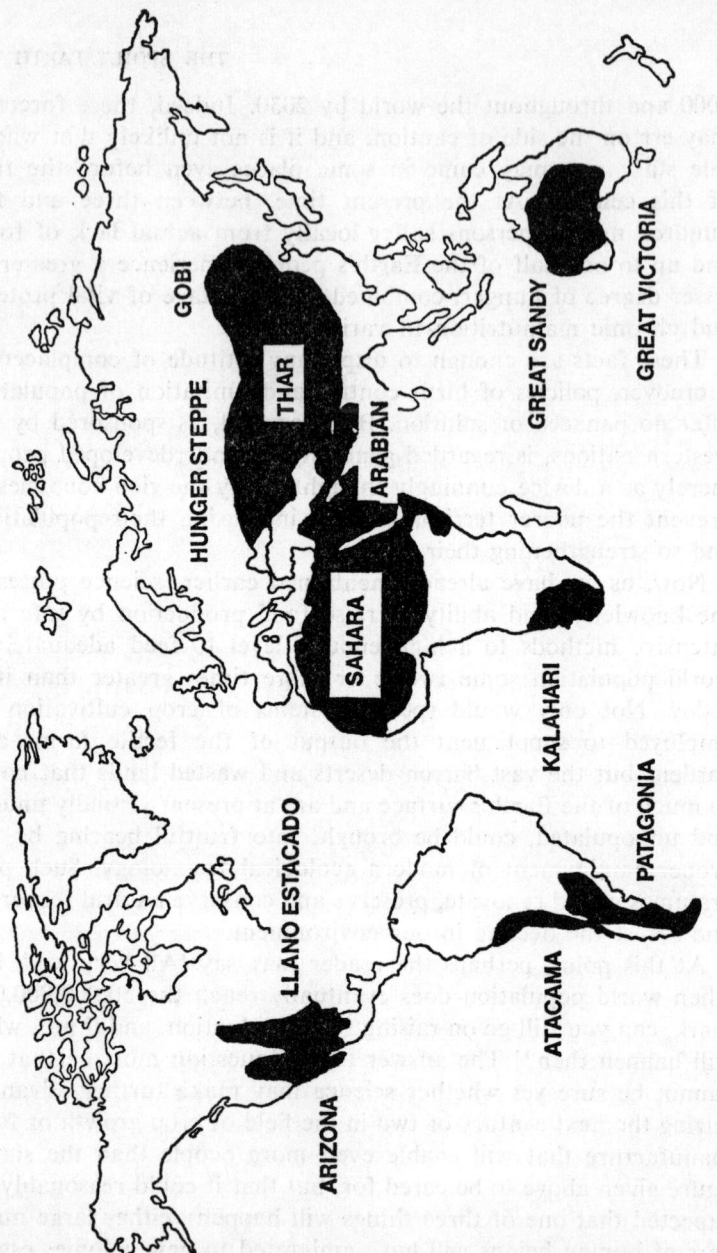

Figure 13 THE GREAT DESERTS OF THE WORLD. A large proportion of the total of these barren lands has been created by man's destructive activities. These deserts are expanding constantly and engulfing neighbouring areas, causing serious droughts, loss of life amongst human beings and animals and much misery and suffering.

folly will have destroyed life as we know it today, and will possibly be replaced by different creatures.

In any event, our planet will be doomed if we do not act soon to preserve our environment and respect and care for all the living organisms that exist on Earth now. Although most of the pollution of the biosphere by industrial wastes, pesticides, poisonous smoke and noxious gases or metal particles may be confined largely to the cities, towns and manufacturing areas or farmlands, the effects of the damage are carried by wind and water throughout virtually every part of the globe. It is a fact that almost no region of the world does not today show evidence of some kind of man-made pollution, even if only in traces so far.

Man's ignorance and greed have been responsible for the extinction of numerous species of animals as well as serious reductions in the populations of others. No less than sixty types of living creatures are currently seriously endangered by threats from human beings, ranging from rhinoceroses to polar bears, eagles to gorillas and whales to wild horses. The list is long and very saddening to read. Plants, too, suffer from pollution and thoughtless destruction. Indeed, the evil is not confined to animals and vegetation but also extends to man himself. Many human beings have died during recent years from the effects of poisons released from industrial complexes or through illnesses induced by modern ways and habits of living.

So the world dies slowly but inexorably while most of us sit by, just like the Emperor Nero did while Rome burned, but playing not upon our fiddles, but on our greedy desires for more material goods. The blame for the present state of affairs may be found entirely in man's bad and senseless treatment of Earth. After eliminating so many species of animals and damaging the forests, soils and waters, his pollutants have brought about a situation where the oceans, seas and rivers hold less life and the soil is becoming incapable of producing good crops unless dosed with massive quantities of unbalanced fertilisers, applied almost haphazardly, with little knowledge of the ultimate consequences, by farmers. Good land is still being seized in industrial countries for building factories. Natural resources are being employed to produce luxuries and comforts instead of basic necessities. Minerals and metals are being used up far too rapidly, with little care for the future. Yet, Earth's reserves are not inexhaustible or limitless, and should be conserved and their utilisation planned, not dissipated wastefully in wanton and foolish greed.

As farmers cut down trees and remove hedgerows they take away the natural protection from the land that prevented erosion and loss of soil. Vast amounts of good earth are blown away by strong winds. The quality of the soil deteriorates because straw from crops is foolishly burned, causing more air pollution, instead of being ploughed back into the ground or turned into compost. The land needs organic material to keep it in good heart – fertilisers alone are not enough. Rain washes out valuable nutrients which are never replaced as they used to be in former times. The destruction of hedgerows also deprives wildlife of places to live and drives away useful and beneficial animals, birds and insects, while the continual application of poisonous pesticides creates a silent and dangerous countryside, with loss of many valuable species which once lived in harmony with man. When trees and woods go, the balance of nature becomes disturbed. Disastrous droughts in many parts of the world have already killed thousands of animals and reduced human communities to penury and ruin.

Surely it is time for man to realise that what he has done, and is doing, wrong. Proper understanding of the serious position would be the first step towards a change of course, with eventual reclamation of the situation by proper conservation measures, elimination of pollution, and respect for all life. If we do not soon heed the writing on the wall, the pace of deterioration will increase, as Earth continues to die, so that finally our planet will be lost to us.

POLLUTION

In practice, pollution or contamination takes many forms. Befouling of the air, the land, and the water are commonplace today and result from man's ignorance of the basic factors that go to make up a balanced world. One of the worst types of pollution is atmospheric contamination. This may not always be immediately apparent, but it is steadily becoming more notable and its insidious effects present serious dangers to us all. As population rises and industrial output, sponsored by the growth in manufacturing favoured by governments, is developed even further, so pollution inevitably increases.

Aerial pollution comes mainly from industrial smoke and gases, but it is also caused by the burning of refuse and the habit of farmers in western countries of setting fire to the straw of cereal crops in their fields. Open hearth combustion of coal in domestic premises adds to the trouble. The engines of modern jet aircraft burn fuel containing hydrogen which combines with oxygen in the atmosphere to produce water vapour. This naturally enhances cloud cover. Large aircraft fly at great heights, where man cannot live without special supplies of oxygen. Water vapour caused by the passage of the aeroplanes remains present at these elevations for much longer periods of time. The effects on world climate are still not definitely known, but some serious implications could arise. Even if the dangers are minimal, the risks are too great to be taken.

Manufacturing industry gives rise to unpleasant by-products, such as poisonous gases and thick acrid smoke. These are passed through tall chimneys into the air above us. The rates of escape of this pollution may be quite slow and every day more noxious material is added to that already emitted. In areas where factories are numerous the air becomes grey with smoke and fumes. Plant and animal life survives, if at all, with considerable difficulty, while the health of human beings is seriously affected. Smog or a mixture of smoke and fog is caused by a combination of these two conditions and is highly unpleasant and gives rise to breathing complaints, bronchitis and lung troubles, as well as other chronic illnesses.

Automobiles are some of the worst offenders of all polluters of the air. The fumes from motor car exhaust pipes not only contain carbon monoxide, a very poisonous gas, but also minute particles of lead. These are swirled about in the breeze or wind or settle in dust on the ground. Lead is extremely dangerous and will attack the brain. The level of pollution by this metal is increasing steadily, chiefly on account of the rising number of motor cars being added yearly to the roads. Photochemical smog arises when strong sunlight acts upon car exhaust fumes and produces a poisonous haze. This problem is serious in Los Angeles, where large numbers of trees, often miles away from the city area or suburbs, have been killed and poisoned. The same dangers have arisen in New York, as well as in Tokyo, where special oxygen-providing machines have had to be installed at regular intervals in the streets of the worst affected localities. People have to run to the machines to inhale oxygen in order to keep alive, so great is the volume of traffic emitting fumes and poisonous gases. In London, too, occasional exhaust smogs can be noted in the centre of the city. Power stations also add to pollution. As towns grow bigger, the need to provide more electricity increases and so the number of power stations rises, and the higher becomes the quantity of gases and thick smoke poured out into the atmosphere. These augment smog and low cloud cover.

Urbanisation inevitably leads to overcrowding, because more town amenities are required and more factories must be built nearby to give work to the inhabitants. Refuse disposal presents additional difficulties, and the air gets less clean as cities expand to accommodate extra people. In the United States, for example, seven out of every ten persons now live in towns or suburbs. Yet these urban areas occupy only two per cent of the whole country. Here, indeed, is an extraordinary example of overcrowding and maldistribution of population. By the year A.D. 2000, it is estimated that ninety per cent of all Americans will reside in cities. Other nations face similar maldistribution, as towns become larger and the rural populations migrate into the urban and industrial localities, in continuous streams.

Air pollution is a root cause of other forms of contamination. All kinds of very harmful particles of dust and gases are carried in the atmosphere and settle upon vegetation, often far removed from the factory areas. Moreover, when it rains or snows poisonous substances floating in the air are dissolved and fall upon the land, where they soak into the soil or enter lakes, reservoirs, and rivers. Rain today, in both industrial and country regions, is frequently dirty and most housewives will have noticed how it discolours washing left outside to dry, if the clothes happen to be caught in a sudden downpour. Plants are stifled by impure air and their stomata are choked, so that they eventually die from lack of nourishment. Dust from brick-making has been known to destroy mature trees. Insects that rely upon plants for their food cannot survive in polluted air and the insect-eating birds such as swifts, swallows and house-martins then find it impossible to obtain sustenance, and so leave the contaminated areas. Certain plants, such as lichens, which are particularly sensitive to atmospheric pollution, soon disappear when the air becomes be-fouled. Various mosses are also good indicators of poisoned air and water, and it has been noticed in Scandinavia that the level of lead in such species has been rising rapidly in recent years. Even in Greenland, where there are scarcely any motor cars or factories, the amounts of lead recorded in snow have risen during this century. This poison is carried by wind and rain from Europe and America to the Arctic.

The prevailing winds in Europe, moving from west to east, take up noxious gases, notably sulphur dioxide, in Germany and Great Britain, and spread the fumes of these poisons in Scandinavia and north-east Russia. Extensive damage has in this way been caused to the coniferous forests in those areas. Not only are the trees killed and new growth checked, but also the death and removal of such great shelter belts will eventually cause a

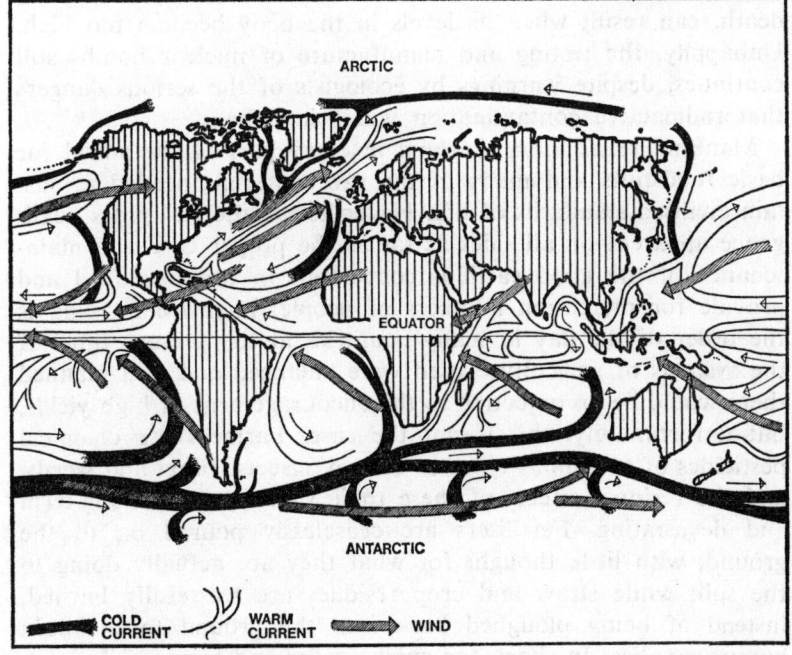

Figure 14 GENERAL PATTERNS OF WINDS AND OCEAN CURRENTS THROUGHOUT THE WORLD.
(Note: Certain changes in winds occur at different seasons)

complete change in the natural life of the region and destroy the function of the vast northern woodlands, which at present break the full force of the cold arctic winds and protect much of Europe from too severe winters. Valuable timber resources are also being damaged beyond remedy. It should be remembered that trees provide building and furniture-making materials, pulp for paper manufacture and other useful items, quite apart from their functions in land conservation and climatic amelioration. In addition, beneficial wildlife obtains shelter in forests and many of these helpful organisms control in a natural manner objectionable insects, plants and other life forms that might present serious dangers to human beings if they were not kept constantly in check by biological means.

Another very dangerous type of air pollution is radioactive fallout, caused mainly by the exploding of atomic and nuclear devices. The effects of strontium 90, a product of such activities, are well known, and destruction of bone marrow, as well as death, can result when its levels in the body become too high. Unhappily, the testing and manufacture of nuclear bombs still continues, despite warnings by ecologists of the serious dangers that radioactive contamination will bring about.

Mankind relies upon the land in every part of the world for basic foodstuffs and many of the raw materials needed to sustain civilised standards of life. Nevertheless, there is gross negligence apparent on all sides as far as the proper care and maintenance of the good earth is concerned. In order to feed and provide for increasing numbers of people, intensive farming is the order of the day in many countries at the present time. If the systems of agriculture used were balanced and well planned there would be no objection to the encouragement of high yields, but unfortunately, this is not the case. Farmers use chemical pesticides of poisonous types to destroy insects, fungi and weeds, and the residual effects of these toxic substances are long-term and devastating. Fertilisers are ceaselessly poured on to the ground, with little thought for what they are actually doing to the soil; while straw and crop residues are wastefully burned, instead of being ploughed back into the ground to maintain humus supplies. In short, for quick profits and temporarily large crops, modern agriculturists rape and abuse the land upon which we all depend. Far more plant food is removed from the soil than is ever put back into it and this causes the eventual break-down of the earth, with consequent erosion and loss of permanent fertility. When soil is abused it ceases to be a living entity and turns to sterile dust.

It is a rule in nature that what is taken out must sooner or later be replaced. Farming the soil means that organic matter must be returned to keep up the health of the land. While it is perfectly possible to grow crops without using soil – in hydroponics – where we can create a viable, self-contained and different sort of ecosystem – when we are cultivating the land itself we should conform to proper laws and not rely upon the temporary results of fertilisers alone, which can never replace or provide the organic matter so vital to permanent fertility. If large areas of forests are cleared, the land often deteriorates and eventually becomes a desert. The ill-effects of reckless and haphazard clearing of tree cover can be seen in the United States, where great 'dust-bowls' were created by destruction of woods and prairies; in Spain, south Italy, and North Africa; in India, western China and the Middle East; and in northern England and Scotland, where the clearing of hill forests has left thousands of acres of nothing but rough grass and bleak moors or denuded highlands. In the English region of East Anglia, ancient forests which formed a natural barrier to strong winds coming in over the North Sea were removed by farmers. This altered the local climate, the condition of the soil and the general balance of the area. Consequently, very serious erosion of good land has occurred as the wind sweeps unchecked along the surface of the ground and carries away millions of tons of irreplaceable fertile top-soil every year.

Pesticides and fertilisers should always be employed with great care and it is far better to make use of natural substances such as pyrethrum, which is harmless to livestock, than rely upon toxic materials. Persistent chemicals not only destroy pests, but also kill and injure many species of beneficial types. Some of these organisms perform the functions of biological controllers in that they are predators of harmful species. It has been found in the United States that spraying mercury compounds to eliminate fungus disease can kill the valuable robin, which consumes numerous troublesome insects and has always been regarded as the farmer's friend. Often, poisonous pesticides are absorbed by their victims, which may then be eaten by other useful creatures which in their turn die of the effects of the poisons. This passing on of poisons through the food web or chain concentrates them and gives them greater lethal potential. Breeding of birds and animals may be halted by pesticides. The eggs of a species can become infertile or the shells may be thinner, thus causing them to break before the incubation period is complete. DDT and Dieldrin are particularly objectionable and have been responsible for the depletion or extinction of a number of kinds of valuable birds, such as the eagles, kestrels and falcons. Defoliant chemicals have disastrous effects on the environment, damaging vegetation and killing wildlife over extensive areas.

In some areas, the levels of contamination by pesticides sprayed on to food crops are extremely high. DDT has even been found in human milk, caused by the mothers eating cereals that have been treated with this chemical. In large amounts, such toxic materials could induce death, and at the least they lead to nervous disorders and lower resistance to certain diseases. Despite its help in controlling malaria, DDT has to be used with great caution, since not only can it have adverse effects on human beings and animals but the malarial mosquitoes themselves can build up resistance to it – or to other similar chemicals – in the course of time.

Refuse dumping gives rise to much pollution of the land. Great mounds of rubbish can be seen in and around cities and suburbs today. These harbour dangerous bacteria and vermin. Birds alighting on them carry diseases far and wide. Yet, refuse can be sorted, some being made into valuable compost for fertilising crops, and other portions utilised in manufacturing processes.

During recent years, there has been a marked increase in the pre-packing of foods and other goods. Many of the materials employed for these purposes do not, however, break down when they are thrown away. This adds to the pollution by refuse. When plastics are burned they release poisonous fumes into the atmosphere. The amounts of indestructible waste are increasing and this means more rubbish and more pollution as time passes.

It is often hard to find sources of uncontaminated water these days. Because water is essential to all life every means to keep it as pure as possible should be sought for. The oceans and seas are befouled by oil slicks, which kill thousands of birds, dolphins, seals and other organisms. Serious disasters of this kind have occurred in recent years off California, near Cornwall, and in other areas. Even in the middle of the Atlantic Ocean thick crude oil has been found floating in huge lumps. Pollution from oil seems likely to increase as more oilfields are opened up in coming years, especially in the middle of seas on the continental shelves. Direct pumping into rivers of chemicals, effluents, wastes and untreated sewage contaminate the water and destroy fish or other life that used to thrive there. The chemicals known as PCBs, employed in paint and varnish making or as lubricants, are particularly dangerous. They build up in the bodies of fishes, which may be later caught and consumed by human beings. Much of the surface water of the world is now polluted with PCB chemicals.

Untreated sewage is another offender, and excessive amounts of it can extinguish life by what is called the process of eutrophication. This means the clogging or choking up of lakes and rivers by a fast rate of water plant growth, so that the oxygen in the water becomes exhausted. The colour of the water ceases to be clear and turns to a deep green shade. Run-off pollutants are caused by farmers and gardeners spraying or applying pesticides and ill-balanced fertilisers to the land, in excessive amounts. Rain washes these into rivers and lakes, with the result that algae growth in the affected waters increases greatly. This is why we can see many lakes, in places such as Switzerland, where the formerly blue water has turned an ugly greenish hue. That country's water is now seriously polluted and must be purified before it can be drunk by human beings. Untreated sewage and effluents or industrial wastes add to the problem. Today, the river Rhine is simply an open sewer, the Great Lakes are moribund, the Danube is seriously contaminated and there are practically no natural waterways in Europe or North America where it is safe to bathe or use the water for human consumption.

The list of water pollution effects could be continued indefinitely. Diseases such as typhoid are increasing due to befouled water. Harmful metals, including zinc, lead, arsenic and mercury are discharged by industrial manufacturers into inland waterways and carried out to sea, where they are absorbed by fish. Birds eating these fish die in large numbers. The contaminated fish themselves have been caught and consumed by human beings with disastrous effects. At Minimata Bay, in Japan, where waste mercury was deposited by a factory into the sea, many people have died from mercury poisoning brought on by eating locally landed fish, while babies have been born deformed with mercury deposits in their small bodies. High mercury levels have also been noticed in fish caught in certain English and American waters. Cadmium poured out as waste from zinc smelting has caused a disease called Itai-itai in Japan. The poison found its way into ricefields through the medium of the irrigation system and the people who consumed the rice were stricken by this sickness. Their bone size was reduced, they could not stand up or walk and they grew gradually shorter in height, while suffering acute pains. Some areas in other countries are also contaminated by cadmium poisoning. Dumping of all these toxic substances into inland waters and in the oceans and seas is a dangerous and serious cause of much pollution.

Contamination is very widespread in the biosphere at present. It may be found even in the far north of Canada, where animals and birds have been poisoned by industrial wastes conveyed thousands of miles by wind and water; in the Antarctic where penguins have died from similar pollution; and in the middle of the vast oceans of the Atlantic and Pacific. No place in the world is safe any more from man's polluting pesticides, poisons, toxic substances and industrial wastes.

THE POWER OF MAN

As the dominant species on this planet, man today feels that he is all powerful and can change the nature of the world. Although his actions do, in fact, alter life on earth and he possesses the means and authority to take over the biosphere completely, eliminating all other organisms in the process that he feels do not bring him profit or wealth, it would be a sad mistake if he really believed that such a course would bring permanent and beneficial results. Pride always leads to a fall. The ancient Greeks were right when they said that the greatest error, which incurred the most serious punishments, was *hubris* or insolent pride.

In fact, all of man's new and important discoveries often appear to bring about more unhappiness and dissatisfaction with life. Our actions on earth may, indeed, change our existence and styles of living, but very often in ways that we may not welcome and do not really want or desire. The present technological age was supposed to make conditions better, but as we can all see, it has in numerous directions made them much worse. The balance of nature has been twisted and upset, many animals have been rendered extinct, the environment has been seriously polluted, the landscape often altered from beauty to ugliness, and the civilisation of which we were once so proud bent to become an enslaving colossus that will crush and abuse its captive populations.

What can be done? The downward trend can only be halted if a number of vital steps are taken by communities and individuals. It must be realised, first of all, the earth is not the property of man alone and is not limitless in resources or potential. The environment should be put before economic and industrial growth and expansion. Pollution must be controlled effectively. People need to be informed fully of the present situation and the dangers it presents. This means education and instruction in ecology and how to apply it in our daily lives. In short, our whole attitude towards the earth and our natural resources will have to alter very drastically.

If there is to be no change in man's general outlook and his actions then the future of the world will be hazardous and unfortunate. Standards of life will decline, raw materials will become exhausted and the overcrowding and pollution will become unbearable. Famines will occur, societies will break down, and poisoning of our waters, soils and air will be inevitable. The need to preserve our planet in a healthy state and to recognise the warning signals now being given by nature must be realised by mankind if life as we know it is to survive. Finally, it should be considered by every man, woman and child that it is his or her duty to conserve and improve the earth which supports us and to guard all forms of life existing in the world, with the object of ensuring a better future for ourselves and our descendants.

The need to care for our planet – which is the only habitat that we have now – is very real. Ultimately every form of life depends upon every other form, so reverence for life is vital. We should stop destroying the earth's soils, plants, animals, water and air, as well as avoid pouring wastes into the environment and using up scarce resources at alarming rates. Natural cycles should be adhered to and materials re-used and conserved. If all of us work together we can preserve and safeguard the world for all life – now and in future generations – but if we ignore the warnings of nature disaster will inevitably overtake us.

Note: Various other forms of pollution may be seen in different areas. These include noise contamination, offensive smells and odours, and visual pollution by the occurrence of objectionable sights or spoliation of areas by unsightly buildings or events. Generally speaking, such kinds of pollution affect individuals and communities more than they do actual damage to the biosphere permanently, but all the same they are a cause of much concern to all persons anxious to preserve the environment in good condition.

CHAPTER FOUR

Man the Dominator

This chapter is concerned specially with the place of man in nature and his relations with other forms of life and the environment. Here we have what is termed human ecology or the study of the structure and development of human communities and societies, how they adapt to their surroundings and conditions and the manner in which they utilise technological methods and patterns of social organisation. Human beings are not, of course, the only social animals on this earth – we have bees, wasps, ants, termites and other species, as well as different forms of rudimentary social groupings in numerous kinds of organisms. But man is at present the dominant world species and has reached the highest and most advanced stages of organisation that this planet has probably ever known.

As a specific discipline, human ecology involves the application of the broad perspectives of the biological sciences to the investigation and study of the wide range of subjects covered by what is often called sociology. It was Darwin's theory of evolution, published in the latter part of the nineteenth century, that really made possible this straightforward and naturalistic approach to clarifying man's place in the world. The first steps in ecological assessment of human affairs were concentrated on the problems of population growth, patterns of economic activities, the reasons underlying the location and functions of towns and cities, variations in diseases and death rates, and the social division of labour, or what jobs individuals and groups usually did and why. The framework of human ecology was built up by such well known pioneer ecologists as F. Ratzel; E. Durkheim, author of *The Division of Labour in Society;* and C. H. Cooley. In Chicago, R. E. Park and his followers carried out extensive work on the subject, publishing in 1925 the well-known book *The City.* Although the majority of the early studies in human ecology were undertaken in urban surroundings it was soon found profitable to employ similar methods in the investigation of other types of societies and groups.

DEVELOPMENT OF CHARACTERISTICS

Ecological studies have made it possible for us to interpret differences amongst individuals and societies largely as reflections of varying environmental and grouping conditions and of the ways in which human beings modify or adapt to changing circumstances. This is not, of course, to overlook inherited characteristics, but to understand how they combine with other factors to produce various life styles. Special observations of tribal groups, for instance, have revealed that connections exist between the gathering or growing of food, the kinship patterns and social ranks, and the size of, or arrangements within communities in villages and settlements. Ecology has, therefore, been able to put forward a broad outline within which the development of populations, environmental adaptations, technologies and the organisation of social affairs have progressed or been moulded and can be assessed and studied in a clear and enlightening manner.

The results of lengthy research in prehistoric archaeology have made it obvious that primitive man obtained only a very poor return for most of his efforts to find food and provide himself with elementary shelter and safety. The rudimentary technology of the Old Stone Age could give human beings little in the form of useful tools or weapons. The environment was dangerous and harsh and life was precarious or short, as well as being full of hazards, such as diseases, accidents, starvation, or attack by wild beasts or enemy groups. Communities in those days were small and dispersed over large areas. Division of labour as it is practised today by age or sex would have been difficult to arrange. With the coming of Neolithic man, however, and the emergence of a settled form of agriculture, better food gathering was secured, and the capacity of the land in particular places to support larger numbers of people was increased by farming. So a sedentary manner of existence developed and there was even the possibility of a small surplus of crops and simple village-made goods over and above the needs of minimal subsistence requirements. Such items could be exchanged with other communities for different products. New techniques could be introduced by local craftsmen and the various social roles within groupings would become more defined and organisation more elaborate.

Neolithic villagers are known to have worked in metals, used irrigation and employed other simple technologies. In general, all these efforts prepared the way for the establishment of early towns, of much greater size than the original villages and possessing some complexity of organisation. Such cities could be supported by the surrounding agricultural regions. In due course, various settlements would acquire adequate forces to embark on military expeditions and so gain control over many of their neighbours. Caravans passed on the primitive roads between one centre of population and another, while small sailing ships maintained contact between places separated by seas. In these ways, quite an extensive trade was built up in the exchange of goods, and supplies could be moved to where demand was strongest.

The pace of life in ancient cities and their territories was slow and leisurely, in comparison to what we are accustomed to today. The early urban civilisations, as well as the later empires and the feudal states of as late as the eighteenth century, were low-energy societies, relying on man-power, domestic animals and elementary machinery to produce their foodstuffs, manufactures and luxuries. The first phases of the industrial changes of the nineteenth century were based on the earlier invention of machinery operated by water and steam power, employing coal as fuel, an innovation which as time passed resulted in vast programmes of industrialisation accompanied by the movement of rural populations into the new urban and factory districts. The process still continues today.

If we look at this chain of events, we can see that each stage is noteworthy inasmuch as it represents some significant expansion over the preceding one. The whole pattern of movement of human beings has proceeded through sequence after sequence in entire series. Sometimes the sere has been interrupted at other times one sere can succeed another, and climaxes (stable conditions for a period) are attained. However, the pace of development has been very unequal in different parts of the world or amongst different societies and communities. No climax has ever proved capable of lasting for ever. Populations increased, both in the sense of their density within given areas and in the territory over which they held sway or conquered and settled. In addition, with the aid of new and improved technologies, human beings were able to develop further natural resources, and make machinery to enhance the efficiency of the exploitation of old ones. This meant that the environment was being enlarged constantly as the ability and aggressive capacity of the societies in question grew. At the same time, specialised social roles developed, numerous groups, classes and strata within communities appeared and the organisation of civilisations became more complex, with many ramifications of interrelationships between sections of the population.

During the present century, the rate of man's expansion has not slackened. World and regional populations have increased at higher rates than have ever been known in recorded history. Technological innovations have proliferated and a new source of energy – atomic power – has been discovered. There have been countless applications of novel materials and processes. Exploitation of the Earth has intensified and the scope of human efforts has been widened progressively. Both on a global scale and within nations, organisational patterns have become far more complicated. All these activities have been accompanied by alternating periods of aggressive warfare and uneasy peace.

The radical and far-reaching changes of the past one hundred or so years, have had marked effects upon individuals and communities in all parts of the world. All the same, there has been great variation in the consequences of technological advances in different areas, some localities remaining relatively little affected and others altering beyond recognition. The consequence is that the successive stages and sequences of history are paralleled by striking contrasts in societies, pushing certain groups forward and leaving other more isolated ones in primitive states. The high-energy communities are driven by desire for change and increases in material wealth or goods; while the low-energy groups still lack initiatives and the impetus to break with their older life styles. Nevertheless, in course of time, the latter may seek to emulate the example of their more advanced fellow men.

Despite all the developments since the industrial revolution, however, no climaxes would appear to have been reached in any human sere which could be considered to be of long-lasting or permanent nature. This situation is in striking contrast to that pertaining to the cases of bees, ants and termites. Here, we also have social organisms, whose societies, unlike those of men, are stable and well regulated and which seem to have attained secure and definite climaxes long ago. Whatever man's permanent climax may be, if any, it is certainly far off in the distant future, when world conditions may well be unrecognisable in the context of today. In addition, human interference with the environment has now placed mankind at a particularly dangerous threshold, which no other organisms have attained, and which could – if the wrong course is taken – throw all civilisation back into the primitive darkness of pre-history or even earlier times, from which all the long climb upwards would have to begin again.

THE UNIQUE ANIMAL

Human beings have been called unique animals because, whilst possessing all the characteristics of other animals, such as the requirements for food, shelter, territory, sex and reproduction, they possess the potential capacity to understand their own roles in ecosystems and to realise the advantages of foresight. Contact between human ecology and animal or plant ecology is most noticeable at the point where concern arises for the viability and structure of existing or new ecosystems. Patterns of living and occupation by human individuals and communities of particular habitats must affect the other organisms and non-living components of such systems. We can think of examples which would include the establishment of towns and settlements, the exploitation of land for food growing, mining or factories, and indeed a whole range of activities, which can alter the dynamics and organisation of ecosystems. Man's technological progress has made it possible for him to bring about very profound changes and modifications of the environment, or even to create artificially-functioning units. It then becomes necessary to adapt human behaviour and living patterns to the new circumstances. Such modifications bear heavily upon general welfare in many complicated ways often extremely difficult to anticipate or foresee. Serious errors have been – and are being –

made in initiating environmental changes by man, and it is the purpose of ecological study to provide a means of correcting such mistakes or preventing them from ever occurring. Because mankind is today the dominant species on Earth and has the power to dispose of the planet's resources and other forms of life much as it may please human wishes or desires, the ever-present question is: will we be capable of using the power we possess wisely and well, or will we make disastrous judgements and thus in the end destroy ourselves and the biosphere in which we exist, perhaps in some future time to be succeeded by a more intelligent and gifted species of quite different type and outlook?

QUESTIONS AND ANSWERS

As the world population of human beings increases and pressures on the environment intensify, many practical questions are being asked daily which require urgent answers that only ecology can supply. For example, development and progress may often clash with the need to preserve amenities or retain healthy and enjoyable standards of living, or there may be difficulty in dividing up scarce resources in the best possible manner. Perhaps it is a matter of draining some seaside marshes to provide sites for building homes for people, to be weighed against the requirement that such areas may be vital to the production of food from marine species existing there. Again, how can the discharge of factory waste or effluents be handled, so as not to damage rivers, lakes or even oceans? Or would it be sensible to construct a large new dam in a certain area, which could provide electricity and irrigation for dry lands, if the effects of such a barrage might be to incur some risk to health and to destroy good fishing grounds existing at the estuary of the river to be damned? These may be large national, regional or community decisions, but similar, smaller-scale questions arise in families and neighbourhoods when decisions of crucial significance affecting welfare and daily living have to be made. The ecological response is always to look for facts – to find out, say, how much of the food energy actually needed for the fishery came from the marshes; what are the alternative ways of disposing of industrial waste materials; or how necessary is the estuarine catch to national and local requirements and whether the dangers to health can be controlled. Individuals and families, also, when they think in ecological terms, will want to investigate and balance the various advantages and disadvantages of different actions and courses in the light of all relevant facts. Guesswork must be avoided, and aside from the element of chance, ecology does not arrive at decisions without a proper scientific probing of every aspect of a given situation.

Man exercises much influence upon the composition of eco-systems since he often removes or introduces new species or non-living elements to them. When the changes are very carefully planned, all may be well, though not in every case since lack of foresight and skilled investigation can bring about quite unusual or contradictory and disastrous results, but only too often the alterations made by human beings are accidental, thoughtless or inadvertent. Serious imbalances frequently occur in such instances. Diversity is important in nature, especially for its contribution to increased stability of ecosystems. Human attempts to create pure species culture, such as in crop fields, in managed fish ponds or in factory-farms, reduce survival ability and heighten the risk of diseases. The more species that may be present the greater will be the adaptability to changing conditions, because of the larger pool of genes and the capacty of adjustment to environment. We can therefore see that it is very risky and uncertain for human beings to depend on, say, only a few varieties of wheat or rice in agricultural production because climatic change or sudden onslaughts of diseases could wipe out a limited number of specialised varieties or strains rapidly. In a similar way, the considerable number of races of men in the world are a real insurance for the future, since if one or more succumbed to rigorous conditions or degenerated irreparably, some of the others might still survive and adapt to take the places of those that had become extinct.

The interaction of energy and materials in ecosystems is of much concern to man. Since in nature the efficiency of transfer of energy derived from sunlight into food and raw materials is low as compared to what may be achieved by machinery, it has often been thought that human beings can improve the process considerably. However, ecosystems vary greatly in terms of production and utilisation, and while extreme strains are clearly detrimental, it is impracticable to lay down one rule for all conditions. Investigations have shown that there is an upper limit to the efficiency with which light can be employed for the synthesis of organic matter on a large scale in natural systems. The best prospects for raising energy use and production are to reduce any limiting factors of physical type and extend the seasons of growth so that light is available for the bulk, if not all, of the annual cycle. In other words, we usually find that much of the sunshine falling on crops may be wasted, or fall at the wrong time. To remedy this state of affairs, involves what we may term artificial controls and managed production, which in turn rely on man's skill and efficiency to maintain them in existence.

Man is a dependent heterotroph, that is to say, he relies upon green plants, immediately or ultimately, for his livelihood, especially for his carbon needs. It is therefore really impossible for him to control the biosphere unaided for his own good, both now and in the future. By this is meant the fact that human beings must have the cooperation of the bacteria living in the soil, the autotrophic organisms which build up food materials from inorganic substances and many other forms of life. Key roles are played by these in biogeochemical cycles, such as the sulphur and nitrogen cycles, and the microorganisms especially are not passive actors in physical and chemical surroundings, but are active participants in regulating their environments. No single organism or population normally has complete control, but when all work together the sum total of any well-balanced and ordered ecosystem will be continuous supplies of the energy and materials required for life. Only too frequently, man seeks to secure temporary advantages by increasing the output of materials, but forgets completely to arrange for an equal return mechanism. One good example of this behaviour is the constant failures experienced in farming in the tropics. A few years of satisfactory crops may be followed by poor productivity as soil nutrients leach away or become unavailable to the plants. In the native forests or savannahs there exist return arrangements for maintaining the fertility of the land, but in imposed agricultural systems this is seldom catered for. Biological recycling is quite common in nature. Nothing is wasted and systems are well ordered. If they are not, then they will die away and be replaced by successors.

Stable and productive environments are essential to man's

well-being. This implies that the principles of ecological succession are of great interest to human beings, because they need the early stages for sources of food to give a big primary output, and the mature stages to ensure the integrity and permanence of the ecosystem. A stable climax can act as the buffer and control for physical forces, such as water and temperature, in the environment. Thus, satisfactory mixtures of early and mature sequences or stages, with good interchanges of energy and materials, will make living standards easy and satisfying. Cropping fields on farms are, in ecological terms, younger sequences, whilst forests are older or mature ones. The agricultural areas are kept in being by man's care and efforts, but the woodlands are virtually self-sustaining and possess natural diversity. It is well understood how the forests prevent soil erosion and afford protection against adverse weather. Man, however, too often looks upon trees as a source of immediate gain, cutting them down to sell their timber or make way for quick profits from annual plants. In the long run, such policies bring disaster and ruin. It is just in such situations that ecology can teach and explain to all concerned what the right course to take should be and how to strike a happy balance.

Data has to be made available to the public to show everybody the real importance of mature components in any ecosystem and their role in stabilising the environment and supply‧ing water, nutrients and the other essentials of life for individuals and communities. To think only of production, without any preservation and conservation, is a highly dangerous outlook. We can see the ruins of once-great civilisations, the occurrence of man-made deserts, and squalid or noisome industrial complexes, which stand as evidence that man has frequently forgotten his heterotrophic nature and the necessity for adapting himself to planetary requirements during his efforts to dominate and control Earth. In short, human beings must work with nature and not attempt to damage or destroy the balance of existence on Earth, if ultimate and widespread disasters are to be avoided.

MORALS

Little progress will be made by the reader in his or her study of human ecology if any suggestion of holistic emphasis is permitted to enter into the subject. The ecology of man is a part of general ecology, just as human beings are dependent upon other organisms and the non-living components of the biosphere for existence. Holism, that is to say the theory that the fundamental principle of the universe is the creation of wholes or complete and self-contained systems ranging from atoms and cells by evolution to the more complex forms of life and mind, belongs to the realm of philosophy and is not a part of science. Morals and customs in ecological thinking are reflexes arising from the pressures and interrelationships of various living conditions. As we know, attitudes and habits change from time to time and vary from place to place. Nevertheless, they do have important bearing on the responses of different individuals and communities to circumstances and influence behaviour greatly. Even animals follow primitive customs and practise a wide number of habits, which originate from the patterns or adaptations imposed upon them by the factors of the environment in which they exist. In general, morals and customs may be regarded in ecology as the products of experience: something is considered to be a 'good' habit because generally speaking it brings beneficial results for the greatest number; while another thing is thought to be 'bad' since it can lead to suffering and difficulty. From the practical point of view, most of these morals or customs have been developed over very long periods, but as conditions alter in every age, so the habits differ and what may have been believed to be right and good in one age may be disliked and suppressed in another. We can recall several examples to illustrate this fact: slavery, war, brother-and-sister marriage, polygamy – but here there is still variation in different areas today – homosexuality, capital punishment, and numerous other subjects. Frequently, various taboos and old customs were instituted initially to guard against inadvertent violations of an ecosystem's stability. Although the ancients had no specific knowledge of ecological principles, yet they did maintain quite often a real sense of the integrity of the environment and attempted to prevent serious damage to it in some cases by imposing prohibitions that would strike fear into individuals and communities, if they transgressed a mandatory and arbitary code. Perhaps in certain ways, such old laws were preferable to the unregulated and careless attitudes towards the world that we see around us today.

CHAPTER FIVE

The World of Animals

Unlike human beings, of which there is only one species, *Homo sapiens,* now existing on Earth, there are very many kinds of animals, ranging from the minute zooplankton through the fishes, reptiles, birds, and smaller and middle-sized mammals, right up to the big elephants and whales, living on the land or in the seas of our planet. All of these organisms have their own special characteristics and may occupy different habitats, but in general, integrated patterns of coexistence and interdependence are apparent everywhere in the animal world. Many sorts of approaches to the study of animal ecology have been proposed and are employed by investigators. Some of these methods will be of little more than academic interest to the reader, since our main purpose in this book is to concentrate on applied bionomics, which can serve definite and useful objectives in daily life. However, it is well worthwhile setting out here the various attitudes and lines of enquiry that may be employed from time to time.

METHODS OF STUDY
(1) *Investigation of particular animal species or groups.* Some very interesting books have been written, such as Darwin's *The Formation of Vegetable Mould through the Action of Earthworms;* Wheeler's *Ants;* Darling's *Herd of Red Deer;* and Nice's *Studies of the Song Sparrow;* as well as thousands of technical papers, on the subject of the investigation of individual species or populations of different kinds of animals, by ecologists and other scientists. Insects, however, appear to have received more attention than most creatures have, perhaps because they can represent both dangers and benefits to crop producers, as well as carrying diseases that injure or kill human beings. The practical value of ecology in the field of insects has been proved

and the knowledge gained from the studies of the various species has been of great economic advantage. There are, nevertheless, some disadvantages to be found in investigations confined to particular animal species or groups, because if efforts are to be concentrated on certain profitable, attractive or dangerous types of creatures, then it is likely – for there are literally thousands of kinds of animals – that other species may well be neglected. Moreover, separate consideration of selected organisms or assemblages in isolation frequently tends to overlook the interrelationships existing between those individuals or groups and others, as well as any syntheses that may exist.

(2) *Studies of relationships existing between an animal and its environment.* This line of approach often puts too much attention on the relationships which arise between animals and the environments in which they live and displays only minimum or secondary interest in the kind of creature under investigation or the factors governing the conditions of existence. Many works have been published on the social life of animals and the responses and behaviour of parasites, most generally under the relationship heading. It is known that when any given animal cooperates with other animals, various phenomena of a social nature appear. The simplest form of these attitudes would be a common stand for defence against enemies. Slightly more complicated would be a division of labour, followed by perhaps segregation of the process of reproduction and the development of castes or classes of individuals. Parental care of the young, exchange of food between a nurse and its charge or *trophallaxis,* and other practices may be seen. With some groups, the number of offspring produced may be in inverse proportion to the amount of care and protection given to them by their parents. In other words, the less the care, the more young are usually produced. This fact is easily noted; a frog or a fish will release thousands of eggs, which result in vast numbers of young creatures, most of which die before they reach maturity, but the mothers or fathers do not normally help or defend their young; whereas a gorilla or a human being will guard and look after their one or more babies and children for several years. In animals, where there are two sexes, courtship and mating behaviour are developed. This precedes actual coition, which thus might be considered in human terms to become a less lustful

and brutish act.

Quite different species do associate for mutual benefit in processes termed *commensalism* and *symbiosis*. Antagonistic relations are also seen, including predatism, aggression, or parasitism, when one species feeds upon another, drives it away or deprives it of food and territory or exploits it in some manner.

(3) *Studies of fauna in a particular locality or area.* Here we have a definite area where the ecologist will spend his or her time listing and investigating the animals which live there, as well as their relations to the habitat in question. Such studies can be valuable in identifying the food chains, of which species of crop pests form parts. The quantitative aspects of cataloguing animals in specific areas and the food chains in which they participate, as well as numbers in local populations, are further significant sections of useful investigations.

(4) *Study of the effects upon animals of particular environmental factors.* This is an analytical approach, usually concerned with physical and chemical influences which can be measured and controlled to a large extent. The actual work, after field observations and collections of samples have been made, will be performed in the laboratory or other suitable place, but there is of course a connection at all times with practical activities. Soils, waters and other materials are assessed, climates studied and recorded, vegetation investigated – all from the point of view of finding out how they affect the animals living in the habitats in question. Of particular importance are temperature, humidity, light and chemical factors. It has to be remembered that in terms of numbers of species most animals are cold-blooded, and therefore the temperature of their bodies is little different from that of the air around them. Physiological processes are affected by changes in heat and cold just as the chemical reactions of which they are composed are influenced. For example, we could illustrate the temperature range in which an animal exists as follows:

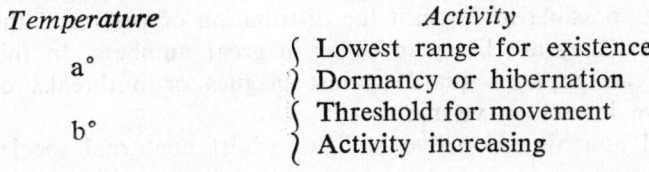

Temperature	Activity
a°	Lowest range for existence
	Dormancy or hibernation
b°	Threshold for movement
	Activity increasing

D

c°		Maximum activity range
d°	{	Decreasing activity
	{	Relative immobility
e°	{	Aestivation
	{	Upper lethal limit

However, whilst this table shows that the area of maximum general activity for the animal in question occurs between b° and d°, with optimum movement at c°, there may well be different ranges and alternatives for maximum activity for the functions of growth, reproduction or sexual excitement, mating, and old age or longevity. In insects, which have different stages in their development and body forms, the optimum temperatures may vary widely for the successive transformations of the creatures. It is therefore relatively easy to obtain information of the effects of heat and cold on particular physiological processes, but it is far harder to find out how a change of temperature influences a whole population in its natural habitat, especially when the fluctuation also affects other organisms in coincidental ways. Land animals present respiratory surfaces to the air, that is they breathe in and out and sweat or perspire, so they lose moisture by evaporation. If carried to extremes these processes can be dangerous, causing dehydration. Rates of evaporation and hazards depend on the relative humidity of the atmosphere. If most terrestrial animals are kept in very dry air they will be unable to control their loss of water and will die. Many small animals, however, live in microclimates where adequate humidity is maintained. A typical example of such a situation would be an aphid existing on a green leaf, which enjoys a local moist atmosphere, even though the air a short distance from the vegetation may be dry. Air currents play an important part in influencing atmospheric humidity, which is, of course closely linked with temperatures. By comparing the requirements of animals with charts, on which are drawn the ranges of temperatures and humidities at different seasons of a year, called climographs, it becomes possible to forecast the distribution of pests and the times when they are likely to occur in great numbers. In this way we can hope to guard against plagues or outbreaks of destructive insects or vermin.

Diurnal animals are active in light, whilst nocturnal species favour nights and crepuscular ones like the times of dusk or dawn. Light also acts as an orientating factor. Ants, for instance find their way about partly by following the angle of incidence of light rays. Illumination also affects migration of birds and body form of aphids.

Chemical factors are prominent in the lives of aquatic animals, but generally exercise indirect effects on terrestrial organisms, chiefly through the soil and flora or vegetation. However, some cases of direct influences are known. Small quantities of cobalt are essential for sheep in their grazing lands, while certain kinds of mites only live on chalk soils. The analytical approach to ecology is today quite a popular one, but the drawbacks are that it can lead to an over-simplification of many problems. The environment is really very complex and does not consist of only a few measurable factors. The significant physical and biotic variables require much more detailed study and control than analytical methods can procure alone.

VARIETY IN ANIMALS

Natural processes ensure that animals seek for and become adapted to the environments in which they live. If they do not in course of time, then the species will die out in, or migrate away from, the adverse conditions. Large herbivores or vegetarian types are a characteristic feature of grassland or savannah regions. Formerly, big grazing birds existed in New Zealand, but today the chief herbivorous species are mammals. Different geographical areas contain ecological equivalents which perform similar functions and occupy corresponding niches, but which are of disparate kinds. Thus we have antelopes in Africa, bison in North America (at least until they were virtually exterminated by the European human colonists) and kangaroos in Australia. There are two types of grazers: running forms, of greater sizes; and burrowing forms, such as ground squirrels, gophers, and prairie-dogs or marmots, noted for the extensive underground 'towns' that they construct. Human use of grasslands generally means the replacement of the wild species by domesticated animals. However, a heavy energy flow normally operates through the grazing food chain or web and ecologically speaking such a move is sound, giving higher production, provided there is no misuse of grassland or savannah resources by overgrazing. Native game species in Africa have built up natural resistance to tropical diseases and pests, such as trypanosomiasis, caused by a flagellate protozoon, carried by tsetse flies (*Glossina morsitans,* et al.) and can survive where cattle and other livestock would perish.

Even in the most limited areas it is possible to find great diversity in natural communities. Pine needles, for example, found in forest litter, have been known to afford a habitat for as many as sixty species of oribatid mites. Ants, which compete actively for supplies of food and for territory, exist in some six thousand species; while the termites or white ants, which abound in the tropics, also comprise numerous types. Beetles are one of the biggest orders of insects, numbering over two hundred thousand species. Bees, wasps and ichneumon flies belong to the same family as ants – the *Hymenoptera* – and are also of many diverse types. Nature is prodigal in the cases of small creatures and encourages the appearance of great quantity and many different species, together with rapid and prolific multiplication rates, to compensate for generally shorter lives and increased liability to death from accident or attack by bigger organisms.

Birds are usually thought of as being of either terrestrial or aquatic types, but zoologically they are divided, in modern terms, into two kinds, the *Carinatae,* which possess keeled breast bones and have the power of flight; and the *Ratitae,* which have raft-like breast bones and are incapable of flying. There are also a sub-class of fossil birds called *Archaeornithes.* Birds outnumber mammals in the world. It is estimated that there are about 130 million land birds breeding in Great Britain alone. Many species migrate over long distances, spending summers in one area and winters in another. These terms are, of course, relative, according to temperatures in the places in question, and migratory birds wish to enjoy equable climatic conditions all the year around, hence their flight from a locality when harsher weather appears and seasonal changes occur. Light and day length have been found to induce migration. A behaviour pattern known as *territoriality* is particularly noticeable in bird species. This relates to competition for space and incidentally acts as a population control. At the start of the breeding season, many males stake out definite areas of their habitats and defend them against any other male of the same species. These territories become their own domains and no rivals are permitted to enter them. Owning and holding a piece of land enables the male bird to mate more easily and secure a nesting place. When mating has occurred, the female generally aids the male in defending the territory. Thus the business of looking after the nest and safeguarding and bringing up the young is conducted without being interrupted by the intrusions of other males or females. The territorial behaviour pattern helps to avoid overcrowding and regulates populations in given areas; it also ensures that all suitable localities are fully settled to an appropriate density.

Most species of animals are intolerant of overcrowding in natural conditions and will often start fighting even before serious competition may arise for energy, water, materials or space. If many struggles occur, the reproduction rate will be reduced. When any marked increase of population takes place, there may be mass migrations out of the overcrowded area, often rather aimlessly or in no specific directions, which can frequently lead to death or suicide. These movements are known to occur with lemmings, and used to happen with impalas in southern Africa, before European settlement of that country resulted in the extermination of the bulk of the formerly vast herds that once ranged over the veld.

Although rivalry between different species is important in nature, observations have indicated that interspecific competition is less significant than the limits imposed by climate, productivity and other general considerations of the ecosystem. Closely related organisms do not very often exist in the same place, and when they do, they generally use different sources of energy, may be active at varying times during the day or seasonally, or perhaps occupy contrasting niches. Should there be many related species present in a single region, the niches will frequently be narrower than when a few such species are observable. Related species quite usually replace one another in gradients as conditions change, say from plains to foothills to mountains. In ecology, we have what is called the *competition-exclusion* or Gause's principle, which results in the separation of closely related species or a reduction in density where such species are able to coexist. This is a biological regulatory mechanism.

Reptiles were the first vertebrates or backboned animals to exist truly on land, and are cold-blooded. Their eggs contain much food material, to support the developing embryo, which does not go through a larval stage. In prehistoric times, enormous reptiles lived on Earth, when the climate was constantly warm, sunny and humid, but today the largest of the main species of these creatures are crocodiles and alligators, with smaller types such as lizards, turtles, tortoises and snakes making up the bulk of the world's reptilian populations. Amphibians are also cold-blooded, but have to return to water for breeding purposes, although they live a good part of their lives on dry land. Commonly seen amphibians are newts, salamanders, frogs and toads. The smallest of Earth's animals are the protozoa. These are microscopic and unicellular, though some may possess more than one nucleus and others do form colonies.

Aquatic animals can be divided into marine, freshwater, and estuarine or brackish water species, on the basis of habitats. There is a very large group of ocean and sea types; a smaller but numerous list of freshwater species; and a lesser group found in river mouths and slightly salty waters. Marine animals, with the exception of certain aquatic mammals and some fish, such as salmon and eels, which usually pass from the sea to fresh water or vice versa, never leave saline conditions. They cannot live in water with a different osmotic pressure or containing a different balance of inorganic salts to that which exists in the oceans and seas. These conditions are known technically as *poikilosmotic,* that is the osmotic pressure of the body fluids depends on that of the surrounding medium; and *stenohaline,* or inability to withstand significant changes in the salinity of the surrounding liquid. Freshwater species can survive in water of much lower osmotic pressure than that which prevails in their own body fluids and are called *homoiosmotic,* but they will not tolerate marked changes in the standard osmotic pressure. Estuarine types have similar requirements to freshwater organisms, but possess the ability to adapt to frequent wide changes in salinity. This capacity is termed *euryhalinic.*

Many different habitats exist in the seas and in freshwater, which may be occupied by wide varieties of associations of aquatic creatures. The bottom living organisms are termed benthic; those of the middle and surface waters are called nekton; and the surface areas themselves are filled with plankton. Benthos are mostly invertebrates and some relatively inactive bottom dwelling fish, with shell living types such as molluscs, barnacles, and periwinkles in shore or littoral zones. Nekton consists primarily of fish, with the addition of mammals including whales, and species such as seals, sealions and walruses, together with the invertebrate squids and cuttlefish. Few mammals, except otters, live in fresh waters, though some dolphins inhabit tropical rivers. Whales spend the summers in polar seas but move into warmer waters for breeding in winter-time. Many kinds of fish migrate against the run of the surface currents as they pass from their feeding to their spawning grounds. Their eggs, which are released in the latter areas, rise to the surface and the larvae are thus carried back by the flow of the water to the places where nutrition is available.

Zooplankton is confined mainly to the warmer and illuminated surface areas and these organisms possess various devices to stop them from sinking. They may be equipped with bubbles of gas, droplets of oil or long spines. Most zooplankton feed on plant or phytoplankton. Jellyfish, however, one of the very few bigger species, are carnivorous and predatory organisms.

Animals are usually classified in two main groups – the invertebrates and the vertebrates. Within these divisions there are many smaller sections. Here is the standard table showing the different families and how they are arranged:

Invertebrates

Protozoa:	Single-celled normally, but sometimes with more than one nucleus or living in colonies. This group includes amoebae, planktons, trypanosomes and malarial parasites.
Porifera:	Sponges.
Coelenterata:	Hydras, corals, sea anemones, jellyfish and floating Portuguese-man-of-war.
Platyhelminthes:	Worms, flukes.
Nemathelminthes:	Round worms.
Annelida:	Worms with segmented bodies, such as earthworms, and leeches.
Arthropoda:	(a) Crustacea: Crabs, shrimps, woodlice, waterfleas and barnacles.
	(b) Myriapod: Millipedes and centipedes.

	(c) Insecta: Cockroaches, locusts, grasshoppers, earwigs, lice, dragonflies, aphids, moths, butterflies, beetles, flies, bees, wasps, ants, and many more species.
	(d) Arachnida: Scorpions, spiders and mites.
Mollusca:	(a) Lamellibranchiata: Bivalved shellfish, such as mussels, oysters and scallops.
	(b) Gasteropoda: Single shelled molluscs, including snails, slugs, limpets and whelks.
	(c) Cephalopoda: Cuttlefish, octopus and giant squids.
Echinodermata:	Starfish, sea urchins, sea cucumbers and sea lilies.

Vertebrates

Pisces:	Fishes.
Amphibia:	Newts, salamanders, frogs and toads.
Reptilia:	Snakes, lizards, crocodiles and alligators, turtles, tortoises.
Aves:	Birds. Adaptations for flight include: forelimbs developed as wings for flapping and gliding, air cavities in bones, weight centralised between wings, no bladder and short rectum, high metabolic rate, large heart with quick rate of beating, very efficient respiration, and constant body heat of 38° to 42° C.
Mammals:	(a) Eutheria: the young develop within the uterus and are born in an advanced state. This is the largest group.
	(b) Marsupials: young born at an early stage and then transferred to a pouch. Kangaroos, opossums.
	(c) Monotremes: Egg layers. Duckbilled platypus and spiny anteater.

The main orders of eutherian mammals are divided as follows: (i) Edentata: American sloths, anteaters and armadillos; (ii) Cetacea: whales, porpoises and dolphins; (iii) Ungulata: hoofed species, such as cattle, pigs, sheep, antelopes, deer, camels, and giraffes; (iv) Carnivores: cats, dogs, bears, hyenas, seals, walruses and sealions; (v) Rodentia: rats, mice, rabbits and squirrels; (vi) Insectivora: Hedgehogs, moles and shrews; (vii) Cheiroptera: Bats; (viii) Primates: lemurs, monkeys, apes, and man.

The above list is not exhaustive, nor does it record all species under any one class or group.

INTERACTIONS AND CONTROLS

In nature, the animal world, so to speak, regulates itself. Most of it, if not all, existed long before the first primitive man began to move about the Earth. There are both positive and negative interactions at work in life and these play important roles in ecosystems. Negative interactions such as succession, competition, predation and parasitism serve to preserve balance, unless they get out of hand, and ensure that growth, occupancy and population distribution are held within the capacity of the land or oceans to bear them. These interactions may be termed mainly inhibitory ones. Positive interactions, which are equally significant, are rather differently directed. They involve cooperation between groups of species. Here we have what can be regarded as a balanced equation, with the negative and positive relationships in life tending to balance one another and impart stability to ecosystems. Simple positive interaction between different organisms or commensalism occurs when one creature permits others to avail themselves of existing shelter or foodstuffs that it possesses, without securing any obvious return for itself. When two organisms or populations aid or benefit each other, but may not be forced to do so for any vital reasons, then the relationship is called *protocooperation*. But if the association is essential for survival it is known by the term *mutualism*. Symbiosis, too, is a mutually beneficial partnership.

Cooperation amongst organisms is very widespread. It can be noted in human and many other relationships. Mutualism, likewise, is important and common in nature. All the positive and negative interactions of animal populations, taken together with the physical and biotic factors of the environment, constitute the controls that maintain and direct the progress of evolution and the development or decline of ecosystems, on a regulated and purposeful basis.

CHAPTER SIX

The Life of Plants

The general method of investigation used in plant ecology is to
clarify and record the distribution of different species and communities and find out how they fluctuate or differ in accordance
with the important factors of the habitats in which they live. The
relationships of vegetation with the environments in which it
grows are studied and detailed observations made of various
influences or characteristics of interest. It is always important,
however, to confirm by experiments the effects of alterations
in conditions and to see if what has been noted down is really
taking place in the field, garden, city or farm. The term 'field'
is frequently employed by ecologists to describe work and investigations carried on under practical conditions, as distinct from
observations and tests done in the laboratory or in some other
theoretical study area. 'Field' can, therefore, cover forests, agricultural land, towns and suburbs, factory sites, deserts, seas,
lakes, and indeed any further applied ecological activities, even
in the home.

FACTORS INFLUENCING PLANTS
Plants and their distribution throughout the world are largely
dependent on the factors of climate, soil and the presence or
absence of other organisms. Climate, of course, relates to weather
and includes temperature, relative humidity, wind, rainfall, and
similar conditions. Soils come under the heading of edaphic factors, while the effects of life forms are grouped under biotic
influences. These are the three chief components of the ecosystem and habitat that will control and change vegetation.

We can observe without difficulty how heat or cold and rain
decide where and when different plants grow and thrive or fail.
Light influences vegetation very considerably and changes in illumination or the extent of daytime will have profound effects on

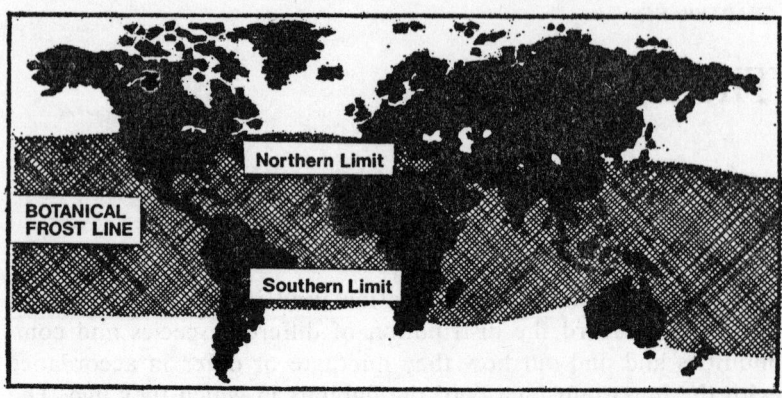

Figure 15 DISTRIBUTION OF PLANTS BY CLIMATIC FACTORS. WHY TROPICAL VEGETATION WILL NOT GROW WITHOUT SPECIAL PROTECTION IN COLD TEMPERATE ENVIRONMENTS. This map shows the northern and southern limits of the botanical frost line, within which frosts severe enough to kill the shoots and branches of tropical plants do not occur, except infrequently.

natural or cultivated plants in normal circumstances. Soils may be damp or dry, and can be well provided with, or short of humus or organic matter. Infertility can be caused by too little lime, deficiencies of other plant foods, excessive alkalinity, and numerous different problems. Lack of water is an important factor limiting plant growth and development. In the opposite way, waterlogging, with insufficient oxygen in the soil, is a serious drawback. Animals trampling an area or overgrazing it may destroy plants. Man, also, often damages the land and kills vegetation. Fire, too, is an agent of annihilation. Strong and vigorous plants frequently dominate and overshadow smaller and weaker ones, which can lead to the death and elimination of the latter. The study of individual plant species or autecology, in relation to their environments, may be simpler to start with, but does not give the wider coverage that investigations of plant communities and their surroundings, or synecology, does.

Vegetation does not possess the power of locomotion on land, or generally speaking, through water or air, as animals, fishes and birds or insects do. Consequently, except by means of seed dispersal, it cannot remove itself to new sites. The importance of soils under such conditions is paramount. Probably the edaphic factors of highest significance in plant growth and development are those of humidity and the content of bases such as lime and others, together with the quantity and type of humus or organic matter. Nevertheless, the influence of these varies greatly in different regions. The amount of lime, for instance, in soils is determined originally by the kind of underlying rock that is present or by the drifts and alluvia deposited above it. With porous soils and high rainfall, lime is frequently removed by leaching, so a sour or lime-deficient soil is produced which is unfavourable or infertile for farming purposes. This sort of land will bear special types of vegetation. Common examples of sour ground are moors and heaths. Here grow bracken, heathers and bilberries, amongst other plants, which tolerate shortages of lime. The soils of such places are acidic, and the bacteria and fungi that normally exist in good land and feed on the organic matter in the earth are affected adversely, so that humus accumulates excessively and the production of nitrates ceases. Thus we will find a lack of nitrogen, that essential plant food, in lime-deficient land.

At the other extreme, some soils contain too much lime and are called calcareous. The lime or calcium is in evidence in the form of fragments of chalk or limestone. Such alkaline ground bears a characteristic kind of flora. In Great Britain, we can see plants such as rockroses, whitebeams and blue limestone grass thriving in calcareous conditions. Vegetation which likes large amounts of lime is termed *calcicole,* in contrast to that which prefers acid conditions and is called therefore *calcifuge.* Alkalinity causes typical symptoms in plants which object to it, notably the sickness known as *chlorosis,* where the leaves turn yellow due to the inability of the roots to absorb adequate iron from the calcareous soil. Availability of nitrates and of phosphate can also be reduced and sometimes that of copper.

Humidity or moisture affects plant distribution in two main ways, where there is insufficient water, and where there is an excess. In most temperate climates, with reasonable rainfall, water shortages are not serious. In arid continental areas, however, vegetation may be scanty or even absent when there is greater or lesser lack of water. Such plants as may grow will be only ephemerals, which live for a few weeks after occasional wet periods. Succulents, such as cacti, which have a low surface/volume ratio and a big, long-reaching root system can survive permanently in many desert or extremely dry regions. Their water relations are peculiar and they possess a special form of acid metabolism that enables them to conserve the carbon dioxide they absorb. Waterlogging of the soil implies absence of oxygen and in such conditions bog vegetation may be seen. Sometimes formations of peat have occurred. If the peat contains lime, luxuriant vegetation can be found, as for example at the mouths of the river Danube or in East Anglia. Lack of lime and nitrogen affect the soil microflora, type of organic matter in the land and the output of plant foodstuffs. In northern Europe, the pine and birch forests grow on soils which are short of lime and nitrogen, but usually have much humus, being called podsols. Broad-leaved forests, however, favour places where the land consists of brown earths of less acidic types.

The chief types of soils and their main characteristics are:

Soil names	Descriptions
Tundra:	Peaty on the surface, with a permanently frozen subsoil.
Mountainous:	Often containing peat on higher flatter land, shallow and stony on slopes, with deeper soils in valleys.
Podzolic:	These are leached soils, that is to say, the rainwater drains through them, carrying away soluble plant foods. Acid to very acid, of low to very low natural fertility, but under good management can be made to yield well. True podzols exist under coniferous forests, while brown and grey-brown podzolic earths are found under deciduous or mixed woodlands.
Red (tropical):	On well-drained sites, these soils are deep to very deep, well leached, moderately acid and bright red to red brown, often with ironstone concretions, and friable. In poorly drained places, the colour changes to blackish and there is a plastic clay, often calcareous.

	A sub-type is very strongly leached, with less bright colouring and lower fertility. This is found under rain forest.
Desert:	Mainly broken rock or sand with little weathering.
Semi-desert:	Chestnut or reddish-brown, ample plant food normally and calcareous near the surface.
Grassland:	Deeper and less leached than podzolic soils, lower acidity and contain more plant foods. In moister areas, the colours are dark brown to dark grey brown. These are called prairie or degraded chernozems. In drier places, soils are black, very deep and go by the name of black earths or chernozems. Very dry regions have shallower reddish black to dark chestnut brown chernozems, depending on temperatures. The deep subsoil often contains calcium carbonate in drier soils.
Alluvial:	Fresh deposits are received every year. These soils are transported or laid down by rivers and floods.

Destruction of natural vegetation by man and its replacement by agricultural crops or plantations are obvious cases of biotic factors influencing distribution and location of plants. Fire is used extensively by primitive tribes to clear land for farming. Indeed, not only semi-savage cultivators employ burning methods, but also some modern European agriculturists, whose haphazard and widespread practices of setting fire to straw left in fields after the harvesting of cereals has damaged trees and hedgerows irreparably in many districts. The North American Indians of former times carried out systematic forest burning to provide parklands for deer grazing. Animals, too, often remove vegetation. Thus the westward advance of the woodlands in what is now the United States was largely kept in check in past centuries by the presence of vast herds of bison, which ranged the great prairies and prevented tree regeneration or further extension of the forest. Some plants, such as trees, succeed in dominating other and smaller species and so affect the character of an area, its soil and its organic matter, as well as its general vegetative cover. Shade is a very important factor in plant competition. Few seedlings, for example, will grow under the dense shade of beech trees. When a new area or soil is colonised by plants, there are always one or more pioneer types which first establish themselves there. We can often see sandy places or sand dunes being occupied by drought-resistant grasses. After a while, these will be followed by more species, as the ground becomes stabilised or fixed by the original occupiers. Humus then gradually accumulates and bacteria and fungi appear. The production of nutrients soon leads to greater fertility. In course of time, such sandy places will become capable of supporting the growth of trees and shrubs, initially of hardier kinds, but later of less robust types. So we will see a steady and gradual improvement of the soil, combined with a definite sequence of vegetation forming a succession of plants. It is these biotic factors that change and improve the habitat in question.

Relations of individual plant species to the environment are very complex because they are always affected by other plants. Dominant types control the growth of subordinate kinds. If, however, the associated species are more or less of the same size, then the presence or absence of a particular type is generally due, not to its ability to survive in the particular locality, but to its capacity to grow in competition. When competition is removed, as for example in a garden, then very large and mixed groups of plants can thrive and flourish. Whilst size is significant in enabling a plant to compete against other vegetation, survival and success depend also on suitable biological equipment. This will include ability to store food and so to grow quicker or for longer periods. Another valuable attribute is the production of large quantities of viable seeds. Margins of success in competition for dominance are very slender, and depend much on continued efforts over many years.

CLASSES AND DISTRIBUTION
Plants can be classified in several ways, but it is simplest to regard them as either *vascular* or provided with conducting vessels and *non-vascular*. The following list will give the reader a clear idea

of the separate classes of vegetation:

Vascular

Psilopsida:	Primitive, spore-bearing species. Only two families survive today, both in the southern hemisphere.
Sphenopsida:	Horsetails.
Lycopsida:	Clubmosses.
Filicinae:	True ferns.
Gymnosperms:	Conifers, such as pines, larches and yews; Cycads, with unbranched trunks and long fern-like leaves. Japanese maidenhair tree; Metasequoia. Seeds are 'naked' and usually borne on cones.
Angiosperms:	Flowering species. Seeds completely enclosed within the ovary. They are divided into dicotyledons with two seed leaves and monocotyledons with only one.

Non-vascular

Bacteria:	Minute organisms of simple structure. Vast number of species.
Fungi:	These plants do not contain any chlorophyll. They are parasitic, or saprophytic (living on dead organic matter).
Algae:	Essentially aquatic plants, ranging from microscopic forms to large seaweeds.
Bryophyta:	Liverworts and mosses.

Plants are distributed throughout the earth in large vegetation zones, which vary greatly in composition and appearance, due chiefly to the effects of climate and soils. We can devide up the world's vegetative cover, or lack of it, into thirteen main sections:

(1) Cool coniferous forest.
(2) Temperate mixed forest.

(3) Warm temperate moist forest.
(4) Warm temperate, drought-resistant woodland.
(5) Tropical forest.
(6) Equatorial rain forest.
(7) Grassland.
(8) Savannah.
(9) Hot desert.
(10) Temperate or cold desert.
(11) Tundra.
(12) Mountain vegetation.
(13) Polar ice caps.

Individual plant species and populations vary very considerably even within any single one of these vegetation zones, according to the land areas in which they may be situated, but generally speaking we can identify the roles of different types and their ecological equivalents in similar but separated places.

Vegetation, of course, as we know, exists in oceans, seas, lakes and rivers and along shorelines, being made up in such cases of species of aquatic plants. The water area of the planet can be divided for the sake of convenience into the following sections:

(a) Seas and oceans, covering approximately 70 per cent of the world's surface. Plant life consists mainly of phytoplankton.
(b) Estuaries and seashores. Phytoplankton, algae, large attached seaweeds, some marsh grasses and other species can be found in these areas.
(c) Rivers and streams, containing phytoplankton and numerous water plants, especially in pools or on banks.
(d) Lakes and ponds. Numerous types of plant life.
(e) Freshwater marshes. Here we may see rushes, grasses, and other water loving species.

PLANT COMMUNITIES
Plant communities are not just simply collections of plants but possess some form of order within them which establishes the relationships between the various individuals and species that make them up. Groups or assemblages of vegetation come into being largely by climatic and other factors which form and condition an environment and dictate the reception that early

colonists may receive when they enter it. Chance plays a big role in determining which types of plants first occupy any site. To this is allied the factor of timing. Favourable circumstances are another important influence, since naturally it is far easier to colonise and expand successfully in good surroundings than it is in bad or poor ones. Dispersal of seed is also significant, especially as to whether the wind, water or animals concerned carry individuals to fertile or sterile spots. Here, competition enters the picture, because if a seed grows beside a superior or dominating neighbour it may never reach maturity, through being deprived of light and nutrients by overshadowing and root contestation.

The environment exercises selection on plant material, eliminating all those individuals or species that cannot tolerate the local conditions. The degree of 'weeding out' may vary greatly, according to whether the habitat is kind or harsh. As time progresses, established vegetation will modify and ameliorate an environment, changing the formation of the soils, and developing systems of layering and dominance, such as tree canopies, shrub layers, ground layers and field layers, composed of appropriately-sized species. Vegetation is by nature dynamic and never static. Cyclic changes and patterns will arise as plants grow, mature and die. Regeneration complexes occur, as new growth develops in phases. Succession is, of course, an outstanding part of community progression through time and groups may be recognised as stages in a sere.

A primary sere or *prisere* will originate on land not previously occupied by vegetative cover. If the habitat was a dry one, the succession pattern appropriate to it will be that of a *xerosere* (Greek, *xeros,* dry), but if it began as standing water then the style would be that of a *hydrosere* (Greek, *hydor,* water). Sometimes, the xerosere and the hydrosere may merge in the course of very many years to become *mesic* or possessing middle-style conditions (Greek, *mesos,* middle), that is to say, mesophytic vegetation, of intermediate type, neither too dry nor too wet. In hydroseres, the limiting factors for plant species are chiefly the depth of the water present and the lack of aeration. The trend of succession will probably be towards the accumulation of silt, thus raising the soil eventually above water level and lowering the water table.

The soils of heaths and moors are generally too acidic to permit tree growth, so succession may not proceed further than the normal covering of shorter species. This represents the climax of the period, often called the edaphic climax. Where physiographic factors, such as erosion occur (these factors hold back succession pattern at various stages, arresting them, so to speak) the conditions may be termed erosion succession. In salt marshes, *haloseres* may be noted, with salt-loving or salt-adapted plants flourishing. These species are called *halophytes* (Greek, *hals*, salt). Coastal plant communities growing on dunes display what are termed *psammoseres* in their succession patterns. The word psammosere comes from the Greek *psammos*, meaning sand. Instability of the sand dunes and the effects of salt spray influence the stages in the sere. When the progress of a succession is held up we get what can be described as a subclimax vegetation. Here, one can think of coppicing, burning, erosion, and other factors, whether natural or man – or animal – induced. When the checks are alleviated, there will follow lesser or secondary successions.

Plant communities can be considered as fitting into the general scheme of vegetative succession:

Community	*Position*
Seral:	Represents some stage or sequence in a succession which is not yet complete.
Climax:	Fully developed for particular time or period. Climatic climaxes are conditioned by rainfall or altitude and edaphic climaxes by soil peculiarities.
Subclimax:	Succession held up for a period by burning, deforestation, coppicing, grazing, erosion or other influences.
Secondary:	Secondary successions following checks in normal patterns.
Artificial:	Farms, gardens, plantations and other devised communities.

CHAPTER SEVEN

Population

Population ecology is concerned chiefly with quantitative events – that is happenings connected with amounts or quantities – that take place within groups or assemblages of organisms and communities, and with those factors of the environment, regardless of kind, which affect and influence the size, growth, composition and life history of societies. The emphasis of this section of ecological research is directed towards numbers. Populations have been called groups of living individuals set in frames that are limited and defined in respect of both time and space. In simpler terms, we could say that they are numbers of people, animals, plants or other creatures residing together or inhabiting particular areas. To study such groups, we have to ask ourselves certain questions: How many organisms are there in the population? Are they all the same or different in biological terms? Where do the organisms live and in what places or ways? These queries, and others, have to be answered if we are to obtain a worthwhile insight into the ecology of populations.

METHODS OF COUNTING
Several methods exist for determining population sizes. Normally a certain area of volume is selected for the taking of complete or sample counts. The local situation will usually decide which form of census should be employed.

(a) *Total count of organisms.* This is the only fully accurate method. Every individual in the given environment has to be recorded. Since this is often very difficult to carry out, it is not frequently used in research studies.

(b) *Total count of a class or stage of individuals.* This method can be employed when it will be enough to know only how many organisms of a specific class or category are present. One could, for example, count all the male tigers in a forest and ignore the females and the young; or record just the adult ants in a nest and leave out the eggs and cocoons.

(c) *Sampling.* A judgement is formed about a population after withdrawing replicated aliquots, that is amounts that will divide the whole without leaving remainders. These constitute, it is hoped, representative samples. If the investigators have a good knowledge of the ecology of the groups being studied and the patterns of distribution of the population are well appreciated, then the method can be very helpful, but only too often unskilled pollsters and others make gross errors in evaluation of the findings.

(d) *Biomass.* Weights of sample portions of the biomass are counted, instead of numbers. These are reported in relation to some defined space.

(e) *Registration.* Once an initial census has been undertaken, the further and subsequent events are recorded at regular intervals. These include births, deaths, movements of population and other happenings. The population size will then be enumerated thus:

Population size = initial size ±

([births + immigrations] − [deaths + emigrations]).

The difficulty here is to get all the changes recorded correctly.

(f) *Marking.* A known number of marked organisms may be turned loose within the habitat. In time, these become distributed throughout the whole area and the community. When samples are extracted, the proportion of marked to unmarked individuals is noted and the total population size estimated as shown in this equation:

$$\frac{\text{Total number of marked organisms released}}{\text{Total population of organisms in community}} = \frac{\text{Total of organisms extracted in samples}}{\text{Total of marked organisms extracted}}$$

The solution is obtained by multiplying the total number of marked organisms released by the total of organisms extracted and then dividing the result by the total of marked organisms extracted. *Example*: 1,000 marked organisms were released and 1,000 extracted, of which 100 were marked: —

$$\frac{1,000}{1} \times \frac{1,000}{100} = \frac{1,000,000}{100} = 10,000 \text{ total population.}$$

(g) *Indirect methods.* Approximate estimates of numbers of organisms may sometimes be made by examining their products. For example, the more dung left around the greater the herd of beasts in a grazing area. One could count the dung daily for a week and if one knows more or less how much excreta one animal passes per diem, one could then calculate the total number of livestock in the locality. Similar observations may be made in respect of tracks for rabbits and birds, frequency of vocal calls, or numbers of houses or huts in villages for human beings. Such methods, however, by their nature, often give rise to errors.

Practical work in the ecology of populations today tends to fall into various main lines of enquiry, such as studies of natural or field groups, of experimental laboratory specimens and assemblages, of communities in towns, and of the functions of categories, classes and stages in the organisation of societies. It is of considerable value to know how populations are distributed, their sizes and relationships, the way they use their territories and how they cooperate with and aggress or compete against other groups. Predation and rivalry between species are also important, as well as how the populations adjust to or tolerate the environments in which they live. In the laboratory, control of the physical and biotic conditions can be achieved and manipulated as desired, but results secured in such circumstances are often at sharp variance with field responses of organisms. Host-parasite interactions come under the heading of epidemiological studies and concern the position of man and other animals as the hosts of pathogenic organisms, causing diseases, such as malaria, sleeping sickness, tuberculosis, diphtheria, influenza, common colds, typhoid fever, and other illnesses. Ecology views the incidence of infectious diseases, caused by micro-organisms, as a part of the general fight between competing life forms that goes on constantly and fiercely throughout the Earth. It is, in fact, war between different species and another sector of the overall struggle for existence. This planet's higher life forms, because they are habituated to existence in our biosphere, can resist many of the attacks of disease-inducing organisms, fighting back vigorously; but the reader may recollect, in H. G. Wells' *War of the Worlds,* how the invading Martians succumbed to the onslaughts of Earth germs, against which they had no inherent resistance. Theoretical population studies, today, are concentrated on mathematical rationalisations, models of the origin and integration of groups, and how societies are controlled by their own functional organisations.

STATISTICAL FACTORS

The three main statistical factors affecting populations, in applied ecological terms, are birth or natality, death or mortality, and dispersion. Various forces bear down upon these events in different ways. The growth, composition and survival of groups of organisms, their sex ratios and stages of development, and their movements, are shaped in greater or lesser degree by environmental changes and the behaviour of the populations in question. Natality increases numbers, but death reduces them. Dispersion may cause temporary reductions which can be made good by immigrations. However, the acquisition of new or better territories may enable the emigrants to increase their rates of multiplication and so eventually the total population will rise often substantially. Natality can be looked upon as potential or actual. Populations in nature produce fewer offspring than their physiological capacities would allow. Moreover, there are very many infertile eggs, numerous aborted pregnancies, and millions of newly born organisms of all types never reach adolescence or maturity every year. Mortality, also, is potential or realised. Different hazards in life, including harsh climatic conditions, predatory and parasitic activities, diseases, excessive overcrowding and other factors give rise to high death rates, often far exceeding those that would obtain in a congenial environment.

Birth rates and death rates in populations are closely linked. High natality might indicate that expansion is occurring, but if the mortality is large as well, then perhaps it is only replacing losses. Similarly, a low birth rate might show that a decline is taking place, unless it is found that few deaths were recorded. What is called the *birth-death relationship* or *vital index* can show quickly the status of a population as regards natality and mortality. This is defined basically as 100 births ÷ deaths, and yields on solution the number of births for each 100 deaths. A vital index of more than 100 shows that a population is growing, but if it is less than 100, then it is contracting. Equality with 100 indicates a static situation. These conclusions, of course, presume the absence of sustained immigration or emigration. Sometimes, when there is a marked exodus of organisms from a group, those left make up the loss by increased reproduction. Should there be a new influx of individuals into a community – and the amounts of food, shelter or territory remain static – then there will soon arise pressures and strains and serious competition, with the result that the death rate will go up.

It has been noticed that as populations pass through their life histories they assume patterns that are termed *growth forms*. The growth form provides a single numerical statement showing how groups have behaved in time. By looking at it we can see a period of positive growth, a period of equilibrium, oscillations and fluctuations, and finally decline and extinction, represented diagrammatically. Usually, rates of growth are at first slow, then rapid, then slow again as the optimum number possible under the given ecological conditions is reached. Once the maximum is attained, several courses become open to the population, assuming that environmental conditions and circumstances are favourable. It may maintain itself with slight variations, it can fluctuate, or it can decline, finally becoming extinct. This last fate usually occurs in nature after climatic disturbances (such as those presumed to have wiped out the dinosaurs many millions of years ago), decreased supplies of foodstuffs, virulent epidemics, or killing in war by enemies. Nevertheless, total extinction is not very common and groups can generally adjust and adapt to all but the most exceptional events. In practice, fluctuations and oscillations are the main regulatory incidents in the growth of populations.

Growth form is influenced by other factors of ecological origin. These are called the *density-independent* and the *density-dependent* factors. Environmental considerations sometimes have the same effects upon groups regardless of the density pattern of their members, and in these cases, the influences are called density-independent; while when the effects vary according to the degree of crowding then they are termed density-dependent.

For example, very hot and objectionable temperatures could eliminate a large proportion of a population living in high or low density conditions. However, the same group might not be vulnerable to predators or epidemic diseases when existing at low density, but very vulnerable at high densities. We therefore find that the most common density-independent factors for terrestrial populations are objectionable temperatures, very heavy or insufficient rainfall, wind and storms, air pressure, light, humidity, and food supply in some aspects.

With aquatic populations, the physical and chemical qualities of the water, light penetration, movements in the water, effects of the substratum and some food shortages are very significant. In the cases of both land and aquatic groups pollution from industrial wastes is also a serious hazard today. Density-dependence factors can either induce growth or cause decline. Overcrowding may reduce food supplies, add more waste products to the habitat, and lead to fighting and injuring of individuals in populations. Fertility can be lowered when there is little room to mate, move or live agreeably. If the environment is altered drastically by excessive density of populations then malnutrition may appear and mortality rates will rise.

MODERN RESEARCH
Ecological investigations into population today are directed towards many aspects of this subject, which has important connotations for modern man, both now and in the future. Important sectors of population ecology include: numerical studies of growth forms; effects of physical factors; equilibrium of groups and under-, optimal, and over-population, as well as densities; productivity, yields and cycles of populations; dispersion, ranges and territories; interactions between host and parasite populations; competition; organisation of social animals, including man, beasts, birds and insects; counting techniques, population integration and control activities. All these aspects of population ecology have economic and other applications.

Very often, it may be desired to increase the numbers of a desirable species in agriculture, fisheries or stockbreeding by means of applied ecological methods. Again, exploited or endangered individuals or communities may require protection or special stimulation, by means of conservation or other actions.

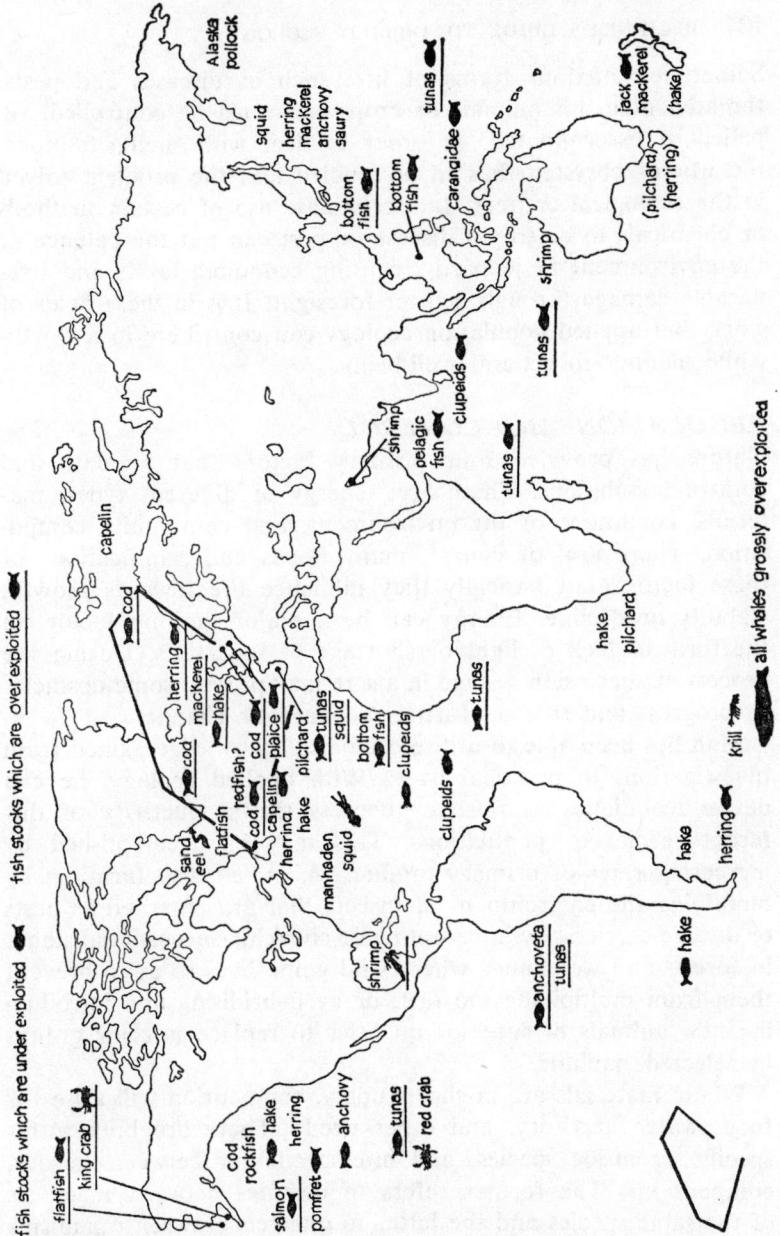

Figure 16 ENDANGERED WORLD FISHERIES. From this map we can see how stocks of ocean and sea species have been seriously depleted by over-fishing and exploitation. However, in some areas certain types of fish are still relatively abundant. The general position illustrates how man is still unable to dispose of his natural food resources properly, and endangers vital fisheries.

Chief British & North European fishing grounds. The northern European nations, having failed to conserve these fishing areas, are now in constant dispute over the declining stocks.

Sometimes, noxious forms of life, such as diseases and pests, threaten man, his animals or crops and must be controlled, repelled or exterminated. In order to deal with such situations, the whole ecosystem has to be studied and the problem solved in the ecological context. Indiscriminate use of certain methods or chemicals to destroy a disease or pest can put the balance of the environment in jeopardy, causing economic losses and irreparable damage through lack of foresight. It is in these fields of work that applied population ecology can contribute in a worthwhile manner to general well-being.

REGULATION AND CONTROL

Nature has provided four primary factors that regulate and control populations. These are: energy of different types, materials, conditions of the environment, and community composition. There are, of course, many facets and ramifications of these factors, but basically they influence life towards growth, stability or decline. Energy can be a major limiting factor, in the form of lack of light or shortage of foodstuffs. During the process of succession a stage in a sere may present some obstacles to progress and so stop further advance or change.

Man has been able to utilise ecological knowledge gained from investigations in practical ways. With applied ecology, he can devise techniques to raise or depress the productivity of different species or populations. This may be accomplished by increasing rates of primary production, in, say, fish farming; by modifying the environment of insects that are regarded as pests or disease-carriers; by interrupting or checking successional stages in forests and woodlands where wild game lives so as to prevent them from multiplying too fast; or by hybridising and introducing new animals of superior qualities to replace inferior groups in selected habitats.

Where materials are in short supply, competition will arise for food, water, territory, and other needs. There are both intraspecific or inside species, and interspecific or between species, competitions. The former refers to disputes between members of the same species and the latter to quarrels between organisms of different species or types. Self-regulation of a single species population of animals may be arranged by fighting which reduces numbers or reproduction rates; while with vegetation, leaf or root hormones are often emitted that inhibit the growth of other individuals in the same spot. In other cases, plants may put out roots through the soil which will kill or depress any seedlings that begin to develop nearby. Not only does this reduce competition, but it also conserves the available water supply by ensuring wider spacing of the flora. We can call these various special arrangements control mechanisms of nature. But should there be two or more similar species, quite well adapted to the same environment, occupying perhaps a single niche or nearby ones, then interspecific competition may intensify greatly. Sometimes one species is ejected or eliminated or has to migrate to another area, or possibly all the species may have to live at lower density and share the local resources in what may be an uneasy sort of balance.

A small number of predators can have a marked effect on populations of primary consumers. If predation becomes excessive then both the prey and the predator may come close to extinction. On the other hand, reasonable predation will stop a prey population from outgrowing its natural resources, thus contributing to keeping balance and equilibrium in the environment. Sometimes, however, the effects of predation are very limited and exercise hardly any regulatory controls over populations. It can be said that any given situation will normally develop according to the degree of vulnerability of the prey to the predator, taking into account the relative density levels of the species and the energy flow through the relationship. The predator spends its energy in chasing and killing the victim. The more successful the prey is in avoiding its pursuer, the greater the amount of effort will be utilised by the hunter. This raises the question: will the energy so expended be compensated by that received by the predator when it eventually seizes and devours the prey? If not, then the effort would be an uneconomic one. The limiting effects of predation are usually reduced but the regulatory influences may be increased, when the interacting populations have had a common history of evolution and exist in a relatively stable and balanced ecosystem. It is not in the interests of the predator, in natural conditions, to exterminate the prey, for it would then lose its future means of support. Violent predator/prey interactions occur most frequently when the relationships are of recent origin, say, on first association of the populations, or if new introductions take place in an area, or in cases where man has disturbed local conditions. Additionally, climatic changes can lead to such interactions.

In practice, most victims can avoid their hunters, if the natural surroundings are favourable. Thus mice in old houses flourish and hide effectively, although the cats which feed upon them eat a certain number and so regulate the population; while game birds breed and live despite the activities of hawks where ground cover is sufficient for them to escape into when attacks occur. Many more similar instances can be called to mind or will be familiar to the reader. In short, nature would not have included the predator/prey relationship within its organisation if it would have led to the extinction of species that form a part of world living patterns. It is man who is the greatest predator of all, killing not only for food, but also for enjoyment and sport, and thus upsetting natural equilibrium.

If, however, an unnatural situation is created, where creatures are placed in unsafe surroundings, then the advent of predators may well prove disastrous. Thus a group of hamsters living in a yard where the concrete flooring was too hard for them to make burrows would soon fall prey to cats climbing over the enclosing walls at night, because there would be no sanctuaries for the hamsters to take refuge in. Often, predators will not hunt or devour prey living nearby, but will look for victims further afield, presumably to avoid attracting attention to their own presence, especially when they live in an area inhabited by other predators who may attack them. For example, a fox can have its earth close by some flocks of poultry kept on a farm or beside a village, but it will not interfere with them. Instead it will go some miles away to another farm or village to obtain its food. In similar ways, human predators such as robbers, burglars and other criminals, will not generally thieve in their own neighbourhood, but may commit their depredations in far-off places, as a simple precaution against detection and capture. Predation does not, of course, always involve only two species: there are numerous cases of several species being concerned and forming a chain of regulatory controls for a number of populations.

Parasitism also exercises control and regulation in populations. Parasites live on or in the host's body. Often there may be gradients of more or less continuous pattern. As Jonathan Swift (1667–1745) wrote:

> "So, naturalists observe, a flea
> Hath smaller fleas that on him prey;
> And these have smaller fleas to bite 'em,
> and so proceed *ad infinitum.*"

Parasitic organisms generally have high reproduction rates and are specialised in structure, metabolism and life history. The environments in which they exist are often peculiar to the different species. Ecological studies have made it possible, in some cases, if due care is taken, for men to employ certain parasites to regulate pests. This is practical biological control, but it demands skilled application or the projects may prove infructuous or rebound upon the initiators. As a rule, in well balanced ecosystems, there is an abundance of natural controls including parasites and predators.

Pest control is an important subject for human beings, because on the safety and protection of agricultural crops depend the welfare and proper feeding of the earth's constantly increasing millions of inhabitants. When man modifies the environment for his comfort and to provide nourishment and materials, he is compelled to defend his dwelling places and farms against the attacks of pests. We call insects, fungi and vermin, which eat and destroy our goods and supplies, 'pests', but of course, in nature, they are simply other organisms. Just like the term 'weed', a pest is really something that is out of place in the human scheme of affairs. What may be a weed or pest in one spot or situation can be a useful asset in another. Modern farming and sanitary services employ chemical pesticides to control competing organisms which seek to eat or damage mankind's goods and health. When used in specific conditions, these have merits, but if broadcast and scattered indiscriminately over the land, towns and seas, such poisonous substances are often highly dangerous, injuring or killing many life forms of great value. From the ecological point of view, non-specific poisons, which can interfere or destroy many kinds of organisms should be very carefully restricted to particular situations and should never be utilised throughout the general environment. Often, biological controls may be substituted successfully for chemical poisons, if ecology is given the chance to investigate the circumstances and make recommendations before noxious substances are applied. In any event, chemical poisons give only temporary relief, they are a mere expedient, and will never afford permanent cures. Similar situations can arise when antibiotics and fertilisers are used indiscriminately amongst populations with frequently unforeseen and disastrous results.

We have mentioned what we call the negative interactions, including predation, competition and parasitism, which exercise controls and regulation over populations. There are also many positive interactions, such as cooperation, mutualism, and friendship amongst organisms. Typical examples are the mutualistic association of leguminous plants and nitrogen-fixing bacteria; the cooperation which exists between coelenterates and crabs; and the close association of algae and fungi in lichens. The relationships frequently so evident between men and dogs, crocodile- or Asian buffalo-birds (plovers) and crocodiles or buffaloes, and sharks and pilot or carangoid fish, constitute similar instances. In such cases, mutual benefits to the individuals or groups concerned accrue, perhaps protection and food, in exchange for certain services of economic or physical value, or even just companionship. In former times, dogs were necessary for hunting and the discovery or capture of wild game for providing meat. Today, they are used on farms, as guards or often for assisting blind or providing company for lonely individuals. The crocodile-birds cleanse the teeth of crocodiles and in doing so obtain a regular diet of scraps; while the buffalo-birds remove ticks and irritating insects from the hide of the buffaloes, eating the pests during the process. Pilot fish may warn sharks of hostile organisms in the vicinity or perhaps guide them towards potential prey. In return, they are given protection and no doubt receive surplus flesh from the shark's kills.

Man differs from other organisms on this planet in that he has developed complex cultures that vary widely one from another according to where he lives on earth. Human beings also possess much greater power to interfere with ecosystems and control events than do the beasts, insects, birds, fish, or the smaller life forms. From prehistoric times, mankind's numbers in the world have been regulated and controlled by war, famine, pestilence, weather, and natural calamities. Today, some of

Above: Sand desert. View of an arid Saharan landscape. *Below:* A pleasant pastoral scene in Colorado – animals and trees well integrated

Plantation and orchard cultivation.
Left: Walnut trees and walnuts.
Above and below: Carob trees and
carob beans – often called St John's
Bread. Tree crops such as these not
only conserve land and ameliorate
climatic conditions, but also provide
large yields of nourishing foodstuffs
for men and animals, giving an
ecologically balanced and permanent
man-made ecosystem

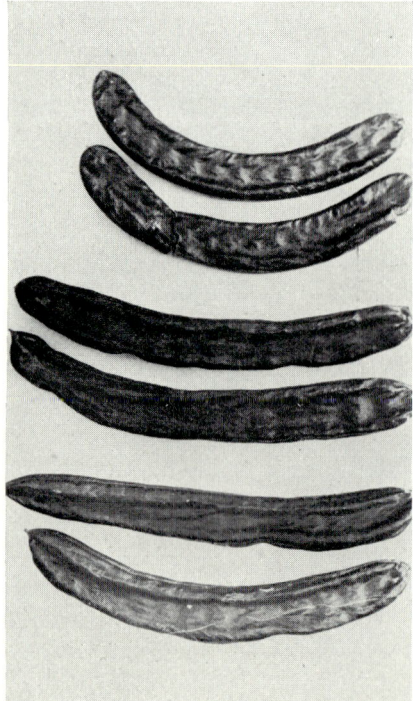

Right: The deep and often stormy expanse of the Atlantic Ocean.
Below: View of naval ships. Each vessel constitutes a self-contained, man-made ecosystem (The letters and numbers on deck of carrier are formed by personnel on parade)

EDUCATION

Left: Children planting a tree near their school in south Wales

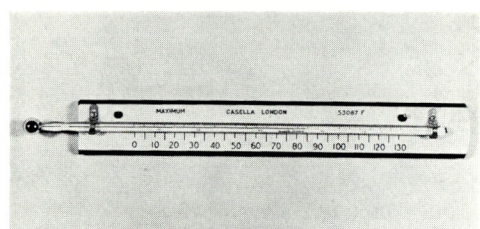

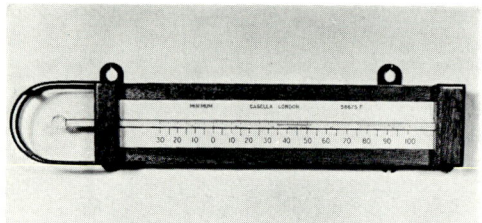

Maximum thermometer
Minimum thermometer
Below, left to right: Wet and dry bulbs
Rain gauge
Rain gauge
Soil sampler

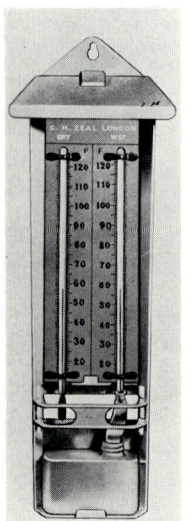

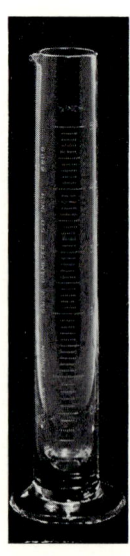

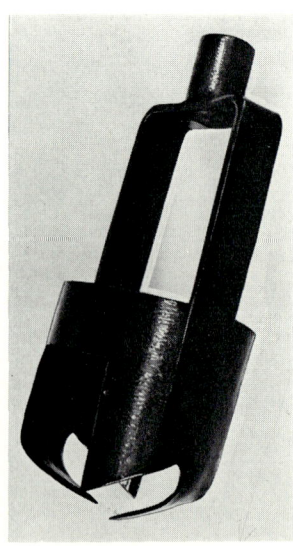

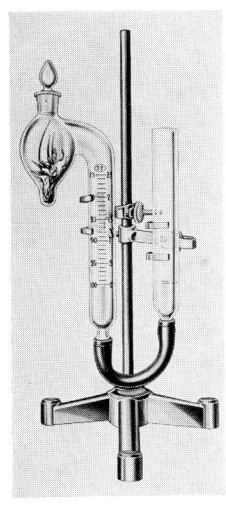

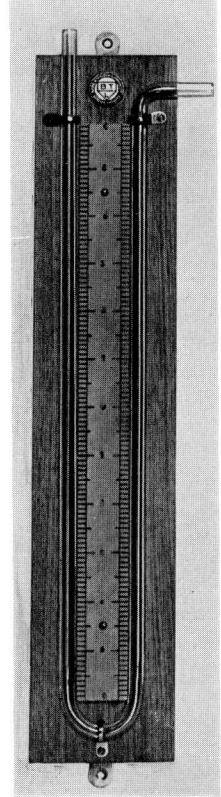

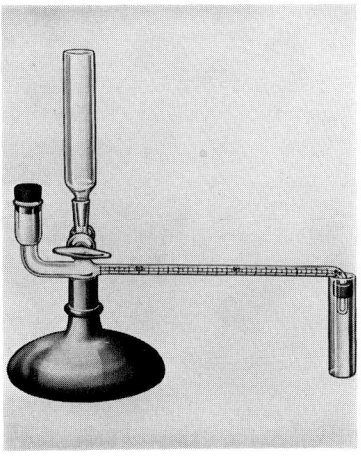

Above, left to right:
Respirometer, Manometer and
Potometer
Below, left: Anemometer
Right: Sunshine recorder

PROTECTION....

Above: Contour strips in Iowa protect farmland from erosion. *Below:* Windbreaks of trees and shrubs in the Great Plains

Above: How grass protects the land and encourages the formation of good soil. Picture shows the effect of special treatment with a stabilisation technique which can rapidly restore eroded areas. *Below:* Mined land in copper area of Chile. Reclamation has been begun by preparing terraces for tree planting

Above: Reclamation of mine dumps in South Africa. The dump in the centre has been flattened and planted with vegetation. *Left:* Reclaiming the desert, Negev, Israel. Picture shows how crops can be raised in the most difficult areas by modern applied ecological methods. *Below:* Tree planting in an industrial area can help to mitigate the unpleasant appearance of factory buildings, as with this Welsh coal processing plant with a screen of young vegetation recently established

these regulators have been partially set aside, perhaps only temporarily, the cynics may say, but nevertheless enough to have allowed the human population to rise at a far more rapid rate during this century than it ever did in the past. We might therefore say that some of the old controls are in abeyance. All the same, nature has not given up, largely through man's foolish and irresponsible conduct in certain areas. For example, the stresses and strains of modern industrial life have led to a great increase in heart diseases, which are one of the biggest killers known to urban populations. Again, machines, such as motor cars and aeroplanes, cause frequent fatal accidents, while pollution of all types accounts for further deaths. Wars still continue, while in the less developed regions, malnutrition, disease and bad hygienic conditions exact their inevitable toll. But still, these factors are insufficient and artificial birth control is now the popular 'panacea' for regulating populations.

What is termed in some quarters the human population explosion proceeds apace. The real problems, however, are those of overcrowding of people into certain areas, where the space and natural resources are inadequate. Vast virtually unpopulated regions remain unused and wasted all over the earth's land surface. Provided ecological methods are employed, the productivity and carrying capacity of the biosphere for man can be increased very considerably without difficulties. There will come a time when the human biomass reaches optimum size and the equilibrium that it then attains with available food and space will mark the limit of population increase, but this period has not yet arrived and will not, on present evidence and calculations, for perhaps two or three hundred years. Before that distant day arrives it is reasonable to suppose that human colonies will have been started on other planets to provide room for any continued expansion.

It must be mentioned, however, that it seems possible that unless human beings change their present attitudes and cease from spoiling the earth, compulsory birth control and other oppressive regulations to stop overcrowding in certain areas may well be developed by some societies. Such laws might be considered to be the ecological equivalents of the customs practised by communities of bees, which decide through feeding patterns how many queens, drones or workers they will hatch yearly; or

E

of the habits of ants and termites, which similarly regulate their populations and classes of males and females, soldiers, and workers, as needs dictate. Whether they might be appropriate to mankind would no doubt depend on the *mores* and cultural outlooks of different human groups.

Not to be forgotten in all these discussions is the process of evolution. By this means, over long periods of time, new species and varieties of organisms are produced. Through evolution as well, ecosystems may survive climatic changes, achieve increasing biological diversity, and exercise modifying influences. Ecological processes combine with geological and genetic processes to shape natural selection. Out of what could be called this cauldron of creation arise new ecotypes, races and species. The ultimate world climax towards which we are today moving inexorably is unknown to us. Perhaps it may be a great future, but quite possibly it will be some overwhelming natural disaster such as that which destroyed the dinosaurs which dominated and flourished on this planet for millions of years long ago, which will bring an end to our age. Alternatively, it could be a catastrophe brought on abruptly or gradually by man's stupidity. Then – in some far distant era – a new and different species of creatures may dig up our long buried skeletons and exhibit them in museums as relics and curiosities or fossils of ancient times.

CHAPTER EIGHT

Ecology in Home and Work

Before proceeding to the discussion of how ecology can help and serve us in our homes and in our work, there are a few important points that we should remember to always bear in mind. These are dealt with under the headings below.

ENERGY AND MATERIALS

The first point concerns energy. The number of organisms – and this of course includes people – that can exist in an area, and the rate at which they live, depends finally on the pace at which energy flows through the local ecosystem, as well as how materials circulate within it, together with the ways in which they may be exchanged with neighbouring systems. Now, non-energy yielding materials circulate, but energy does not. It just flows. All the various materials or substances of which we are made or composed can circulate or pass many times between ourselves and other organisms as living entities and nonliving entities. In other words, each atom of matter may be used over and over again. We can see this happening as people and animals are born, develop, die and return to the earth. Plants grow, nourished and supported by that earth and become food for human beings and other living creatures that eat them and excrete the waste to be used as manure for the next lot of plants. So a cycle exists and continues turning endlessly. Energy, though, is not like that. On the contrary, it is used once only by organisms or populations, being converted into heat, and is subsequently lost from the ecosystem. Once it has passed you cannot recall it in nature; you must look for a new lot. Life, in fact, is maintained by the continuous inflow of energy, and in our case this gift comes from the light of the sun – situated, by the way, some ninety million miles distant – right outside our biosphere.

The one-way flow of energy is a general phenomenon in nature

131

and depends on the operation of the laws of thermodynamics. The first law states that energy can be transformed from one kind into another, but cannot be created or destroyed. For example, we can change light energy into the potential energy of food. The second law stipulates that no process involving a transformation of energy will take place unless a degradation of energy from a concentrated form to a dispersed form occurs. Some energy is always dissipated into unavailable heat energy, so no complete transformation from one form to a different one can ever be entirely efficient, in nature. The interaction of energy and materials in ecosystems is a matter of importance to ecologists. The one-way energy flow and the circulation of materials are two vital principles that must always be kept in mind by students or practitioners of environmental biology. All organisms and all habitats are affected by these matters.

Simplified energy flow diagrams can be prepared, showing the flow of energy between living units. We can see from these that only about half of the sun-light that falls upon green plants is utilised in the process of photosynthesis, and just a small proportion of the absorbed energy, perhaps one to five per cent, is converted into food energy. The total assimilation rate of producers in any ecosystem is called the *primary production* or *productivity*. This is, in fact, the whole amount of organic matter fixed, including that used up by plant respiration during the period in question. We term the organic matter stored in the plants' tissues, over and above the respiration, the *net primary production* or *productivity*. It is this net quantity that represents the food potentially available to other organisms. Now, when plants are growing rapidly under very favourable conditions of light and temperature, the respiration may account for as little as ten per cent of the gross or overall production pattern, thus giving a net productivity of as much as ninety per cent. But, in normal conditions this figure would be very exceptional. The average amounts obtained in nature are far lower. In mechanical terms, the general net production is inefficient and could be regarded as a poor return.

We know that once food or materials have been accumulated in plants they then have to be transferred through other organisms or processes before the final products eventually become available to civilised man. Food chains normally involve several stages of eating and being eaten, as well as manufacturing and packaging. At each transfer of energy, losses occur. Naturally, the shorter the food chain, the greater will be the available food energy. So we can see that many current agricultural and connected industrial processes are highly wasteful and prodigal of valuable energy. This is why more men could survive on a given area of land if they functioned as primary consumers and producer-managers, rather than as secondary consumers only, high up in the food chain.

The basic unit of energy best suited to applied ecological purposes is the kilogramme calorie. This is defined as the amount of heat required to raise one kilogramme of water by one degree Celsius. When we consider the various trophic levels or stages in the food chain, we find, on the average, that the reduction of

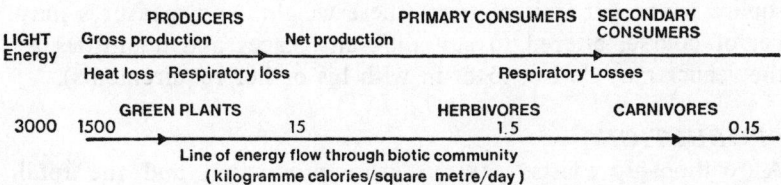

Figure 17 Energy flow.

energy flow with each transformation appears to be about two orders of magnitude at the primary level and after that about one order of magnitude (an order of magnitude means a factor of 10). So, for example, if 1,500 calories of light energy are absorbed by a square metre of crop plants daily, in a temperate zone country, some 15 calories could be expected as the net plant production. 1.5 calories would be reconstituted as primary consumers or herbivores, and 0.15 calories as secondary consumers or carnivores. Indeed, the amount of production in food terms, after successive transfers, is quite small. In practical life, a food chain can seldom have more than three or four links or stages, or the consumers at the end would starve, so great is the loss along its length, should it be unduly prolonged. The position is shown in Figure 17.

The sum total of organisms at each stage in the food chain is a biomass. We already know that such collections are referred to as standing crops. The standing crop biomass is very much influenced by the size of the individual organisms composing it. For instance, a biomass of algae would contain far more organisms than would a biomass of wheat plants of equal weight. Now, generally speaking, the smaller the organisms the higher the rate of metabolism or chemical change per unit of weight. Consequently, it will be obvious that one kilogramme of algae will be far more productive than a similar amount of wheat plants. Alternatively, we could say that one kilogramme of algae is worth several kilogrammes of wheat plants in energy flow, despite its far smaller size. In terms of net food production, a farmer could secure as much material from mass cultures of algae, by harvesting at frequent intervals, as he could from a grain crop which can only be reaped after a lengthy growing season of several months. We can express standing crop biomass in terms of calories per square metre, and productivity as calories per square metre per unit of time (these weights and measures may be, of course, altered to suit different places and quantities as the reader may desire, to fit in with his or her requirements).

PRODUCTION

A relationship exists between gross production and the total of respiration which we see occurs during the energy flow through a biotic community. It is useful to know about this because it helps ecologists to understand the total function of the ecosystem and to predict future events. In a steady state ecosystem, where a climax has been attained, it may be assumed that production equals consumption over a given period, should exports and imports – or output and input be equal, or non-existent owing to self-sufficiency, as when we have a self-sufficient climax situation in the ecosystem.* It is important to estimate balances over reasonable periods, since winter and summer variations, or even weekly and daily ones, can occur. However, steady state or stable ecosystems can take such fluctuations in their strides. But if primary production and consumption by organisms are not equal, so that organic matter in the ecosystem either becomes depleted or accumulates, then the biotic community will probably change through the process of ecological succession.

Observation of the production and utilisation rates of com-

*For example, the Inca Empire in South America, which had no trade with the outside world.

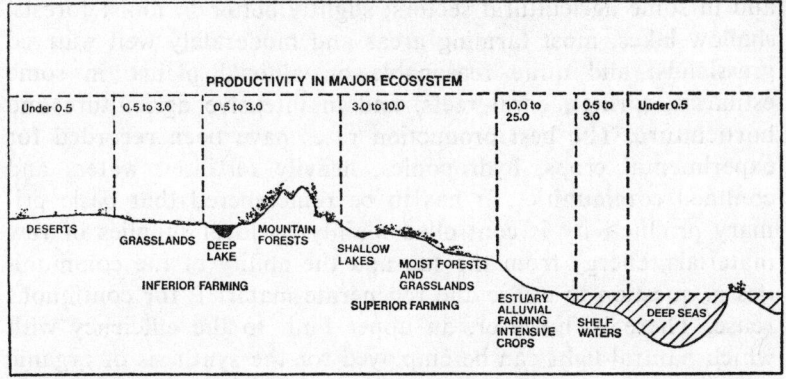

Figure 18 How natural primary productivity rates are distributed. The figures represent grammes of dry matter per m² per diem, as indicated by average daily rates of gross production.

munities will therefore inform us whether they can be looked upon as stable and balanced – in other words safe investments – or whether they are on the point of changes which can be either for good or bad. If production is less than consumption serious and bad times to come are indicated, with a decline in the ecosystem. On the other hand, if production is greater than consumption a surplus and increased disposable assets will be available. In any event, both cases point to change and the need for corrective measures.

Production may not always be confined to simple food chains, such as grass-cattle-men, or vegetation-rabbit-fox, or phytoplankton-zooplankton-whale, because there are also other parallel chains, or energy flows. We have grazing food chains, where grazing animals or herbivores consume standing crops; detritus food chains, when dead organic matter is broken down and consumed by millipedes, woodlice and worms, as well as by bacteria and fungi. However, all these chains are generally associated intimately. How they exercise their detailed influences and what proportions of the total energy flows through each will depend on the different kinds of ecosystems.

Rates of productivity in nature vary greatly throughout the world. They are lowest in deep oceans and deserts; poor in grasslands, deep lakes, continental shelf waters and mountain forests and in some agricultural sectors; slightly better in moist forests, shallow lakes, most farming areas and moderately well watered grasslands; and quite reasonable on alluvial plains, in some estuaries, springs, coral reefs, and in intensive agriculture and horticulture. The best production rates have been recorded for experimental crops, hydroponics, heavily fertilised waters and confined communities. It has to be remembered that basic primary productivity is controlled mainly by local supplies of raw materials, energy from the sun and the ability of the communities in question to utilise and regenerate materials for continuous reuse. There is, however, an upper limit to the efficiency with which natural light can be employed for the synthesis of organic matter. At present, the average standard of farming throughout the world is very poor: grain output, for example being only about 20 kilogrammes (approximately 44.1 lb.) per hectare (2.47 acres) daily. It seems evident that man's best hope of increasing food production rests with efforts to reduce physical limiting factors and extension of the seasons of growth, so as to ensure that sun-light is made use of for a longer part of cultivation cycles.

Relatively large amounts of carbon, hydrogen, oxygen, nitrogen, potassium, calcium, magnesium, sulphur and phosphorus are needed for primary production. These are called the major nutrients. In addition, smaller quantities of what are termed the minor nutrients are required, such as iron, manganese, copper, boron, zinc, sodium, molybdenum, chlorine, vanadium and cobalt. Such elements move through cycles, passing from the non-living sections of the ecosystem to the living sections, and back again. The processes are continuous and intricate. Common examples, which will be familiar to many readers from elementary biology studies, are the sulphur cycle in aquatic environments and the nitrogen cycle in terrestrial conditions. Quite often, different organisms, which do not constitute links or stages in man's own food chain, play vital parts in ensuring that adequate supplies of the elements noted above are present in ecosystems. We may mention here such examples as those of the guano-excreting and fish-eating birds of the west coast of South America; certain shellfish, which are not normally eaten by human beings, but which return detritus rich in phosphates to estuaries; and many seemingly uneconomic plants which still assist consider-

1 SIMPLEST FORM

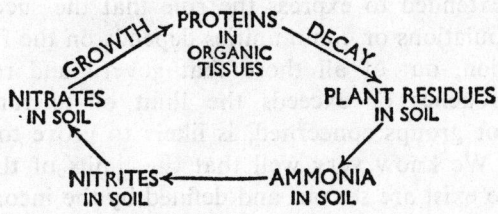

2 MORE DETAILED VERSION

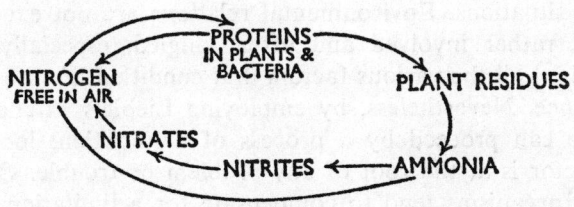

Figure 19 NITROGEN CYCLE. How the element nitrogen circulates in nature.

ably in maintaining the composition of the air that we breathe every day of our lives.

LIMITING FACTORS

Any factor that tends to slow down potential growth, whether in individuals or in communities or even at work, may be said to be a limiting factor. We can see limiting factors all around us in our daily lives. The expression limiting factors was first formulated by Baron Justus von Liebig (1803–73) a German chemist and a pioneer in the study of the use of fertilisers in agriculture. He was impressed by the fact that growth was often limited by whatever essential element might be in short supply. Liebig's *law of the minimum* stated that the rate of growth is dependent on the conditions or nutrients present in the least quantity in terms of need or availability. In ecological questions, the concept is usually extended to express the rule that the success of individuals, populations or communities depends on the fact that any one condition, out of all those that govern and regulate life, which approaches or exceeds the limit of tolerance for the organisms or groups concerned, is likely to prove to be a limiting factor. We know very well that the limits of the biosphere in which we exist are set out and defined by the incoming energy of the sun. In similar manner, the various local ecosystems in which we dwell and work, possess certain combinations of influences that inevitably place further limitations on the structure and functions of all of us, and indeed of all sentient and living organisms.

The value of the concept of limiting factors is important, because it gives the student or practitioner of ecology a door through which he or she can enter into the investigation of complicated situations. Environmental relations are not exactly simple, but rather involved and often tangled, especially at first glance. Not all the various factors that condition life are of equal significance. Nevertheless, by employing Liebig's extended principle we can proceed by a process of elimination, looking for what factor is at the root of any problem or trouble. Quite frequently, organisms tend to compensate for a limitation in some way by endeavouring to overcome a particular handicap. This can happen in such cases as those of blind men and women, who develop a keener sense of hearing; plants growing in low light intensities which reach maximum photosynthetic activity at depressed levels of illumination; or old and decrepid tigers which can no longer chase after animal prey and so turn to man-eating.

INDICATORS

Ecological indicators provide the first signals of the approach of changes or difficulties. It is therefore essential that ecologists should be keen observers, ready to sense and pick out what we might call early warning signs. Rangers and farmers, for instance will find that the decline of certain rarer species of plants in their pastures, which are sensitive to overgrazing by livestock, will indicate that it is time to remove their animals to another area before serious damage can occur to their grasslands. Advance warnings of pollution in rivers and streams can often be detected by noting a diminution of the number of fish species present in the water. Signs of impending troubles in the home, in workplaces or in human organisations may frequently be noticed by careful observation of the detailed behaviour and attitudes of individuals and groups. The list can be extended indefinitely. Experience and study show how we can utilise ecological techniques to recognise and correct situations involving limiting factors or difficulties before they become too critical, by keeping first of all a keen look-out for any indicators and then applying remedial action without delay. In the three instances noted above, the species structure, in the case of overgrazing; the diversity ratio, for pollution; and the behaviour patterns, for domestic and labour problems, are crucial criteria. It is possible to construct a sensitive index appropriate to every situation on which observations and signs can be recorded. Such indices will be of great help in formulating ecological assessments.

Three important points should always be borne in mind when considering indicators and limiting factors in applied ecology. First, you need coordinated field observations, combined if possible with some experimental testing; secondly, though conditions in two areas may appear similar and the same organisms may exist in both, this does not mean necessarily that the environment corresponds exactly in each instance; thirdly, though individual or rare types can make good indicators, you should check their behaviour against that of larger groups because there can be appreciable differences between the responses of single units or species and populations or communities; and fourthly, societies or communities can adapt to conditions or perhaps compensate in some ways, whilst individuals may not be able to do that. This is because the general rates of functioning over considerable parts of any gradient of conditions may remain the same, even though the composition of the groups in question may alter.

It is very noticeable that where environmental conditions are harsher or enervating, such as in desert or arctic localities, or even in less arduous circumstances, the rates of function of the organisms living in these places decline in accordance with the limiting factors present. So we can see why many men resident in hot climates are classed as lazy or apathetic, or why work in such areas proceeds at a more leisurely pace. Again, societies that have enjoyed a softer and more luxurious standard of life may well lose the capacity for labour and become effete or degenerate. Such behaviour patterns indicate that stability of the biomass is adversely affected, and the functioning rates will begin to oscillate and fluctuate often violently, with marked loss of balance and equilibrium.

ASSESSING PROBLEMS

When you decide to adopt an ecological approach to problems, the first thing you must learn to do is to take notes. Ecology is a scientific discipline and as such, is concerned with facts. These cannot be properly recorded unless written down in some organised manner, because human memory and observation are invariably forgetful and often faulty, so that although we have seen an event or viewed an occurrence today, tomorrow it may assume a quite different form in our recollections. Consequently, all ecologists make extensive and careful notes on their studies and tests. As time elapses, these records build up into a valuable and useful history of cases.

Various ways of making notes exist, and all have their merits. The important point is that they should be accurate, legible, and written up in a manner that is easy to follow and presents the facts in concise but adequately detailed and very clear form. Ecologists are often called in to assess particular situations, and after surveying and recording the conditions, position, and circumstances obtaining on the site, they may make diagnoses and appropriate recommendations to solve problems, ameliorate conditions, or suggest improvements. The following form of appraisal is adapted and simplified from a combination of methods that the author has employed in field work, so that it can be used by beginners to record relevant information in ecological style or to serve for note taking when carrying out a preliminary survey of any given situation that might be considered for applied ecological attention. Once you have got all the basic details entered up, you may be able to study and work out some possible answers to the questions that are at issue.

FORM OF ASSESSMENT FOR ECOLOGICAL SURVEYS OF GENERAL OR PARTICULAR PROBLEMS

Note: This form is designed for the preliminary survey and detailed recording of situations or conditions. It is intended to provide a means of noting in an organised manner all relevant information that might be used in assessing and studying problems for which applied ecological solutions may be appropriate.

PROBLEM:

(Enter here a brief description of the situation or problem confronting you.)

PART I – Ecology

(a) *Site:*

(This refers to the place where the situation or condition exists.)

(b) *Present circumstances:*

(List the sere stage or climax conditions. Depending on the nature of the site, record the surroundings in terms of vegetation, dwelling area, neighbourhood, place of work, relevant facilities, and characteristics of the environment.)

(c) *Life forms:*

(Note types and behaviour patterns.)

(d) *Habitat factors:*
(i)   Climatic:
(ii) Physiographic:
(iii) Edaphic:
(iv) Biotic:

(How much you record here should be judged according to the kind of problem to be solved. If it concerns home conditions, then obviously the physiographic and biotic influences will be most important; while for a work situation or difficulty these factors will also be very significant, together perhaps with the climatic circumstances. For farming or gardening, the edaphic features will play a prominent role. Lists of probable factors to be kept in mind are given at the foot of this form.)

(e) *General:*

(Record briefly any limiting factors, indicators, previously un-mentioned adverse or favourable influences and further or general comments on the situation or problem.)

PART 2 – Historiology

(f) *Background:*

(Give an account of how the present situation or conditions appear to you to have arisen in the form of a short history of events. *Important note:* Do not, however allow this section to colour your eventual findings unduly, since inevitably some pre-judice might enter your story. Scientific judgements must always be free of bias and based only on facts considered impartially.)

(g) *Action:*

(State any actions already taken which alleviated, intensified or left the problem or situation as it is now.)

PART 3 – Economics

(h) *Economic factors:*

(Mention the economic considerations that may bear on the matter in question. These will vary from case to case, but may touch on such items as income, expenses, commitments, money available, markets, costs, and other financial aspects, as well as possible profits and losses.)

PART 4 – Subject Investigation . . . (Enter name of subject.)

Note: This section concerns the particular problem or situation in its context as a specific subject. Thousands of different circumstances may arise, but each one should be allotted correctly to its appropriate discipline under this heading. For example, cases may be designated as domestic, business, agricultural or gardening, personal, appertaining to work, sport, or crafts, livestock, marine or freshwater, behaviourial, health, youthfulness, adolescence or senility; architectural, urban or rural, neighbourhood, community, social, pollution, educational; and a host of other subjects, where of daily occurrence or of long-term nature.

(i) *Subject factors:*
(List all factors and conditions affecting subject in question from general and technical considerations and note facilities available or drawbacks which are obvious, as well as needs and requirements that may not be fulfilled.)

PART 5 – General

(j) *Any further factors:*
(k) Views of any persons concerned with or likely to be affected by results of survey:

PART 6 – Report

(Give here a factual and impartial assessment of the situation or conditions from an ecological point of view, after considering the recorded information.)

Recommendations:

(These should only be entered when all factors have been taken into account and the report evaluated and should be of a practical and useful nature, with alternative plans listed, if possible.)

List of some habitat factors:
(a) Climatic: rainfall, humidity, wind, temperatures, light; (b) Physiographic: elevation, situation, slope, erosion, denudation, condition, drainage, waterlogging, neighbourhood, noise, pollution; (c) Edaphic: soil, humus, acidity and alkalinity, moisture, water, salinity, infertility; (d) Biotic: human and animal activities, vegetation, pests and diseases, health, behavioural patterns.

The reader will note that the form is of a general and rather comprehensive design, in order to cater for a very wide variety of problems or situations. It is by no means difficult to modify or adapt it to particular needs or to prepare similar forms specially intended to suit certain investigations or studies. Students of applied ecology are recommended to do that and to draw up their own record papers based on the method set out here. Obviously, if you are anxious to prepare plans for a new garden or home, employing an ecological assessment in order to secure the best results, your enquiries will concentrate on different points to those that would concern persons seeking for solutions to matrimonial, domestic or business problems, or an individual anxious to evaluate his or her future career prospects. We should, therefore, tailor our investigation procedure to suit our subject. This is not difficult in applied ecology, which is the most comprehensive and broadly-based discipline that is available for studying life and our environment and needs today.

DIFFERENT ECOSYSTEMS

It may seem strange to many human beings to be told that they live in ecosystems and their daily lives are governed by various natural or artificial factors, often quite beyond their personal control or knowledge. Yet, these statements are simply formal assertions of our true position in the world. Although ecological factors and processes may vary in relative significance and importance in different environments, we know that physical influences play a major role in controlling groups and populations or even individuals, while biotic pressures also exercise considerable sway over all organisms. Succession, competition, tolerance, aggression, species composition, productivity and limiting factors loom over our heads constantly. The impact of man on the biosphere affects the stability and the patterns of our existence, making us happy or miserable, rich or poor, and fulfilled or frustrated.

Let us consider some typical ecosystems, both natural and artificial:

Seas and oceans

These are the most biologically diverse of all ecosystems, for phytoplankton abound in the surface areas of salt water, and life, in some form or other, extends to the greatest depths. Marine organisms exhibit incredible variety. Tiny plants possess floating devices to keep them within the upper layers of the water, while deep-sea fish have huge mouths and vast stomachs. Much sea food is harvested from the continental shelves to supply human beings, so these regions constitute important sources of protein and minerals for man and his domestic and farm livestock. Moreover, oilfields exist under the sea bottoms in some places and energy from these deposits is becoming available to industrial civilisations.

The oceans act as giant regulators that modify land climates, help to maintain the content of carbon dioxide and oxygen in the air at satisfactory ratios, and provide under lunar influence the tides that scour the shores. The deep sea is also a reservoir of valuable minerals that have been washed down into it from the continents.

The dominating factors in sea and ocean ecosystems are physical ones – waves, currents, tides, saltiness, temperatures, pressures and light intensities. These influences act to determine in great measure the composition of the biological communities and groups, which themselves affect the balance of the bottom sediments and gases in solution. Man only skims the surface of the seas and oceans, in his capacities as sailor, fisherman, oil driller, diver, or sportsman. Many mysteries still await solution in the vast and unexplored ocean depths. There may be found great mountains, huge and virtually deserted plains and perhaps many strange and unknown organisms. To the landsman, the sea is a difficult and harsh ecosystem, but to those who live beside it or voyage upon its surface, something of the grandeur and stability of this still largely undiscovered sector of the biosphere becomes apparent.

Estuaries and seashores
Here we have many diverse ecosystems with distinct ecological characteristics and conditions of their own. Physical factors are variable in river mouths and shorelines, but supplies of foodstuffs are often far better than in the deep seas. Typical examples of such ecosystems are rocky shores, sandy beaches, mud flats, salt marshes, deltas at their outermost reaches, coastal bays and

similar areas. Salinity of the water is seldom constant, owing to tidal action. Energy flow is maintained by the movement of the water which promotes rapid circulation of nutrients and food materials and removes the waste products of metabolism. Plant and animal species living in estuaries and along shorelines are usually of diverse nature. We can find phytoplankton, algae, seaweeds, eel grasses, mussels, crabs, seabirds, seals and sealions, numerous kinds of fish and other organisms in these ecosystems, often comprising very big populations. Unfortunately, man's activities are causing serious damage to estuaries, especially by converting them into open sewers for industrial or domestic wastes. Sometimes, they are reclaimed and houses or farms laid out on the new-formed land. Reefs, dunes and grassed marshes often protect shores against tides and waves. Interference with these features may bring about serious natural disasters, such as flooding and coastal erosion. The study and investigation of estuaries and seashores is a rewarding occupation because the variety of life forms and different habits of the organisms existing there are extremely fascinating and interesting.

Lakes and ponds

Lakes and ponds may be of seasonal or permanent types. Some lakes are very ancient, many dating as far back as the last Ice Age, which culminated about 18000 B.C., and a few even beyond that time. Generally speaking, the diversity of species is lower in fresh waters, with wider distribution over regions, than in salt waters. Lakes and ponds usually possess a *littoral* zone, with rooted vegetation, along their shores; a *limnetic* zone of open water containing plankton; and a *profundal* zone with deep water where the fish normally live. The upper portion of a lake in temperate regions becomes temporarily detached from the lower part, owing to differential heating and cooling, during summer and winter. The top section is known as the *epilimnion* (Greek, *limnion,* lake) and the bottom section is termed the *hypolimnion*. The zone around the dividing line is called the *thermocline*.

The supply of oxygen in the hypolimnion can become depleted and that of nutrients in the epilimnion greatly reduced. During spring and autumn, as the whole body of water approaches the same temperature, mixing will occur again and the entire ecosystem will be rejuvenated. Such changes are quite noticeable to lacustrine dwellers. In bodies of standing water, primary production will depend on the nature of the basin itself, the inflow from the feeder sources and the size. Shallow lakes are normally more fertile than deeper ones. Serious problems have arisen in many lakes due to man-made pollution. Vast quantities of sewage, industrial waste, effluents, ill-balanced artificial fertilisers and pesticides from farms, and other rubbish are channelled or poured into lakes yearly. Such contamination causes death of fish populations, excessive growth of algae and some other aquatic plants, and fouling of the water, with lack of oxygen content very apparent.

Many impressive artificial lakes have been constructed in different areas by damming rivers or forming reservoirs. Aquaculture is practised in some countries, especially in Japan and China, where large yields of algae, fish and shellfish are secured from managed bodies of water. In Bengal, when the rice paddies are flooded, it is customary in certain areas to place fish fry in the fields. These grow to maturity while the rice plants develop and when the crops are nearly ready for harvesting and the farmers drain their lands before reaping, the fish are collected for eating. During the time the rice is growing, the fish provide aeration of the irrigation water by swimming amongst the stalks of the plants, devour objectionable insects and also deposit manure. Thus the farmers obtain two crops from the same area.

Freshwater marshes
These are naturally fertile ecosystems which are not exposed to tidal action. Periodic fluctuations in water level generally occur, with fires occasionally burning off dry rushes and grasses at certain times of the year. It is correct that marshes are often the breeding grounds of mosquitoes, disease-carrying snails which are alternate hosts to the parasitic trematode worms causing the dread sickness of bilharziasis, and other malignant organisms, but they also provide accommodation for useful waterfowl. Rice growing and water gardening are, of course, artificial forms of freshwater marsh ecosystems.

Deserts
Arid and semi-arid regions receive not more than ten inches of

rain yearly. There are both hot and cold deserts, depending on the latitudes in which they are situated or the elevation above sea level. Desert vegetation generally consists of some ephemeral plants which take advantage of occasional rain showers; shrubs with short thick branches and trunks and small tough leaves, with periods of dormancy; and succulents, such as cacti or euphorbias. There may also be some mosses, lichens and blue-green algae that remain inactive in the surface of the ground, unless aroused by the meagre rainfall at certain times. Desert-adapted reptiles and insects that can withstand aridity are noted for their impervious integuments and dry excretions. Some rodents, which are nocturnal in habit, thrive in arid situations, without drinking water. Other animals, such as camels, carry a store of water in their bodies. When human beings have lived permanently in the true desert since ancient times, they have undergone certain physical modifications in structure to enable them to cope with the harsh conditions. The Bushmen of southern Africa, with their large buttocks for storing moisture and nourishment, are examples of this type of adaptation.

Desert soils are frequently fertile. If water can be brought in to irrigate them, large crops may be obtained. However, a word of caution is necessary here. Many irrigation projects have failed because when a large volume of water is poured out over the desert sands it may bring vast quantities of salts in with it, or cause saline materials to rise up from lower layers of the ground beneath the new fields. Such high levels of salinity are fatal to agricultural plants. The chief fault lies in the methods of irrigation: the water is channelled on to the sandy land and then allowed to stand there until it soaks away. Research work carried out in recent years has shown that if the irrigation water is passed fairly rapidly through the fields it will not leave objectionable salts behind in quantity. Moreover, with this method, what small proportion of water is left in the ground after an irrigation will condense in the ground and form vapour between the sand or soil particles. When night comes this vapour turns into fresh dew. The next flushing with more irrigation water will sweep away any salt residues. By utilising such a system in desert areas, good crops can be raised without any fear of noxious salts accumulating.

*   *   *

Tundras

Although these areas are known as barren grounds, a surprisingly large number of organisms manage to exist in the cold and harsh surroundings. Vegetation consists of lichens, grasses and sedges. There are many shallow ponds, as well as the adjacent ocean, which provide additional food. In the Arctic tundra regions, thousands of breeding migratory birds and insects appear during the summer. Resident animals include caribou, bears, wolves, reindeers and musk-oxen, as well as lemmings and marine creatures. The Antarctic continent is noted for its penguins. The limiting factor in these frozen and ice-bound regions is heat.

Grasslands

As the name denotes, grasses occupy and dominate these ecosystems. The vegetation ranges from tall and short species to bunch grasses and turf or sod formers, with underground rhizomes. Well-developed grassland communities will contain types which grow at different seasons of the year – some in summer and others in autumn and spring, thus maintaining production and ensuring good coverage of the land. Quite often, herbs or forbs (small plants) and some woody plants are associated with the grasses. In places where trees and shrubs occur at scattered intervals or in belts and groups alongside stream banks, the ecosystem is termed a savannah. Soils in grasslands are more fertile generally than those under forests. This is because the production of organic matter takes place more rapidly and frequently, as the leaves of grasses fall and decay, quickly forming humus. Large herbivores were the characteristic fauna of grasslands. Man has, however, destroyed all these great herds of former times and turned most of the world's grasslands into cereal farms or ranches for cattle and other farm livestock. This has not been an unwise move, in ecological terms, but the trouble begins when overgrazing is permitted. We are probably all familiar with the disastrous results of this practice, which has caused many serious catastrophes such as the 'dust bowl' of the United States, much of the droughts of West and southern Africa, and the erosion and permanent ruin of vast areas in India.

Forests

Woodland ecosystems are many and varied, ranging from coniferous and deciduous temperate zone forests to tropical rain and equatorial forests in warmer regions. The critical factor in the distribution of tree species is moisture. Moreover, forests take long periods to establish and mature. In the northern coniferous forests the number of species is fewer than in temperate and tropical woods. Spruce and fir are much in evidence in cooler regions, while a whole range of species are found in cold and warm temperate conditions. In tropical forests, which include both broad-leaved evergreen vegetation, growing with the help of abundant rainfall, and deciduous forests, which lose the foliage from their trees in the dry season, many lianas or vines and aerial plants may be seen clinging to or climbing up the stems and branches of large trees. It has been noted in tropical rain forests that there are more species of plants and insects present in a few acres than there are in the entire fauna and flora of Europe, so great is the native diversity in such places.

In all forested areas patterns or gradients of vegetation are apparent as one proceeds from sea level to greater elevations, caused by temperature changes and incidence of moisture. Fire and mass cutting for timber are perhaps the two greatest enemies of forests. Unfortunately, during his history, man has destroyed and ruined millions of acres of once-productive woodlands. This is because human civilisation has always attained its highest levels in regions where forests and grasslands merge. Such areas may be called the forest edges, and they gave man excellent positions in which to build up his communities. In our time, more attenion is being paid to the value of trees, but in past centuries massive destruction of woodlands occurred in North Africa, the Middle East, India, and many other regions of the world, leaving behind eroded and barren countrysides which still persist today. Forestry, as an applied science, is very important to mankind. It is vital to replace all trees cut for timber and raw materials and to increase woodland plantings. Moreover, many tree species bear valuable nuts, beans and fruits which are excellent sources of food for men and beasts. Finally, forests perform an essential function in protecting water-sheds, providing windbelts for homes and crops, and stopping the ravages of soil erosion.

*　　　*　　　*

Towns and cities

In industrial countries today far more people live in towns and cities than reside in the rural areas. Less-developed lands are following the examples of the more advanced states and a continual process of migration from farming districts into urban surroundings can be seen on every side. No abatement of this movement of human beings would appear to be in sight. As the towns and cities and their adjacent factory districts swell and overflow, so the crowding and squeezing of the inpouring millions become intensified. Yet, the attractions of the brighter lights and artificial pleasures of urban life still go on beckoning to the relatively unsophisticated peasants and pastoralists of the fields and ranges. This situation may surprise many people, if they ever pause to think about it, but most of us take the phenomenon for granted. Nevertheless, we are actually witnessing one of the most significant stages in human succession patterns that has occurred in historical times.

No town or city is static. Although they are man-made artificial creations, kept in being by the labours and services of countless millions of human organisms, they are viable ecosystems moving towards or away from climaxes. We know from archaeological investigations that great and important cities have flourished and existed for long periods during past ages. Many have decayed and all that remains of these are a few ruins partly covered by sand or jungle. Perhaps this is the inevitable end of all cities, for being artificial ecosystems, they can vanish and crumble almost overnight, should some sudden catastrophe or change of conditions dictate evacuation or abandonment by their inhabitants. The point at issue here, which should be noted by the reader, is that city and town ecosystems, by their nature, are delicate and precariously balanced and any shift in equilibrium will cause their ageing and death. Within cities we can find many niches with different classes and groups inhabiting them. Division of labour is also very apparent. These are, of course, signs of maturity and as long as the vigour and energy of the population are maintained, survival prospects are favourable, unless external factors intervene to alter the situation.

Suburbs

As habitats for human beings, suburbs were intended to provide the best of two worlds – proximity to towns with added facilities to impart some luxury to life, and the fresh air and pleasant surroundings of the countryside. Unfortunately, in many instances, the city has intruded into the suburb and brought factories and industrial squalor into the midst of the semi-rural and quiet gardens and houses of that formerly peaceful environment. Nevertheless, suburbs do provide a slightly more natural existence for modern man. The mixture of houses, parks, small woodlands and gardens creates a more relaxed atmosphere and induces less erratic behaviour patterns. On the other hand, the very extended dimensions of these environs give to their residents some sense of aimlessness, and the close and neighbourly atmosphere of a village is quite lacking in most cases. The common complaints of human beings living in suburbs are loneliness and often boredom. Commuting between the domestic niche and the work niche can also be tiring and prodigal of energy. In nature, man as an individual would be well acquainted with about one hundred other persons, including his family, friends and associates. Such a group is of manageable proportions and within the comprehension of the average human being. In modern industrial life, the individual is thrown, often alone and without family support, into a much bigger circle of generally anonymous and perhaps unfriendly persons, maybe of different habits, customs and behaviour. The shock and confusion that this ordeal creates build up into open or concealed attitudes of resentment and dislike.

It is very interesting to observe the difference in behaviour between urban dwellers and country or village residents. The latter are usually much more relaxed, friendly at first meetings, and quite sure of their identities. Here we do have, of course, an ecological problem of quite considerable dimensions, arising from the pressures, stresses and strains of twentieth-century city life. The reported loneliness and boredom of the suburbs do not appear to have spread to the animals which are migrating in increasing numbers into these habitats. Because shelter and food are available in appreciable quantities in suburban gardens, copses, parks and hedges, in the case of the shelter requirements, and in the houses' refuse or garbage bins and municipal dumps as far as the food need is concerned, great concentrations of all kinds of birds, of mammals such as rabbits, hedgehogs, rats and mice, and even foxes, have made their homes in suburban areas. There, they are largely safe from predation by man, such as the hunting that they suffer from in the countryside, and from the poisonous sprays and dusts that farmers now scatter over fields and woodlands in ever-increasing quantities, as well as the fierce fires that are lighted every summer and early autumn to burn straw stubble in agricultural areas in many districts, and which destroy hedgerows and shrubberies. Suburbs are definitely developing ecosystems.

Farms and villages
These ecosystems may be grouped together, since they both represent sub-climaxes. The natural climax vegetation of most agricultural areas in the world would be either deciduous forest or grassland and savannahs. In medieval and earlier times, farmers lived in villages and went out to work in their fields every day. This was because life was generally speaking unsafe and raiders or attackers might appear at any moment. As existence became more settled and the dangers of surprise by enemies lessened, so it became possible to reside permanently on one's own land. The farm then could be considered as an extension of the village community. Agriculture, which can be taken as covering the allied activities of horticulture, animal husbandry, orchard work, and many other primary rural industries, is an artificial ecosystem, kept in being only by man's constant activities. Should these be relaxed or abated, even for a short period, the fields and orchards would speedly revert to natural conditions. The sub-climax would accordingly resume its place in the ecological succession, and in due course the sere concerned would attain its normal climax vegetation, leaving no trace of the man-made aberration that once existed under the name of agriculture.

Farming, as an artificial ecosystem, cannot withstand in general serious calamities, such as droughts, bad wind erosion, and other catastrophes, which cause biological collapse in the crops and lands. This is partly because many patterns of agriculture are built up mainly in opposition to nature, in relatively short periods, and do not possess any resilience. Natural ecosystems, on the other hand, except for short-term aquatic ones, take very many years to develop their climaxes. It has been estimated that primary succession on some sand dunes may extend over up to one thousand years; and in mature forests about two hundred years; while secondary succession on grasslands might need approximately fifty years for completion. Despite the fact that long-term successions may suffer many interruptions in areas due to climatic cycles, storms, fires and other effects, natural ecosystems are fairly resistant to extraneous physical forces, although the directions in which they may be pushed by such events are not entirely predictable.

FINDING YOUR NICHE

We have discussed quite a wide range of applied ecological material so far in this book, and the general principles and uses of environmental biology should now be familiar to the reader. Consequently, a few questions that a beginner might put to him- or herself at this juncture could be appropriate. By undertaking, so to speak, a short examination of how each of us views his or her niche in the ecological scheme of things, we can both obtain a clearer understanding of our exact positions and collect some ideas for further enquiries. Here are some suggested questions to help us locate our individual niches.

1.   Can you recognise the particular ecosystem in which you live?

2.   What are the physical factors of your environment?

3.   What biotic factors affect your surroundings?

4.   What kind of habitat do you occupy?

5.   Does the niche that you have acquired (a) domestically, and (b) at work, satisfy you?

6.   How do you cooperate with your species and with other species?

7.   What are the limiting factors that bear most heavily upon you?

8.   Are you aware of indicators of forthcoming changes in your ecosystem's succession pattern?

9.   Is your capacity for tolerance good or poor?

10. Are aggression and competition apparent in your general life?

11. How do you assess your productivity?

12. Could you adapt or modify your living pattern to changes in the environment and the community?

13. Do you find that you become more satisfied when you know why things happen and what the reasons are for changes?

14. Do you think that the earth should be maintained as a home for all species of organisms or for man only?

15. What do you feel about pollution?

16. How do you view population increases and the distribution of people throughout the world?

17. Do you consider it desirable that individuals should produce more food themselves, thus living as primary consumers, rather than staying in groups of secondary consumers?

18. In what ways do you feel you could use ecological techniques in your daily life and work?

19. Would the broad and comprehensive viewpoint taught in ecology be useful to help human beings live more happily?

20. What do you think are the chief contributions that applied ecology could make to your life and future?

21. Should ecology be taught more to children in their homes and in their schools?

22. Are you prepared to recognise that man is not all-powerful and must cooperate with nature?

23. Considering your niche in your habitat, what could you do in ecological terms to improve (a) your own circumstances, (b) those of your neighbours, (c) of your community?

24. If you are not happy in your present niche, have you thought of how you would go about finding another one?

25. Prepare an ecological assessment of your present situation and conditions, and a recommendation for moving yourself into a new niche.

26. Record all the facts about a particular problem and work out alternative solutions in ecological terms.

27. Are you interested in conservation?

28. Have you ever studied, even cursorily, the societies and habits of animals, particularly the social types?

29. What do you feel it is that distinguishes human beings from other social organisms?

30. What is your view of your own and your family's future prospects?

31. Do you think your community or society is (a) progressing, (b) static, (c) declining?

32. If you could spare up to half-an-hour each day, would you be agreeable to sit quietly and think over problems in ecological terms, recording your enquiries and assessments?

33. Do you believe that applied ecology could help you to make better decisions in private affairs, work, or public matters?

34. Would you like to continue more advanced studies in environmental biology?

35. What strikes you as the most important point you have learned from reading this book up to now?

CHAPTER NINE

Ecological Studies and Applications

While it may be very interesting and instructive to read about applied ecology, the beginner will not make sufficient practical progress in his or her studies until efforts are made to carry out some field work. Many hundreds, if not thousands, of helpful experiments and observations can be made of different organisms, groups and populations, the ways in which they behave, and how they respond to environmental conditions and changes. This is all extremely fascinating and exciting, since one is directly concerned with nature and the impact of individuals and societies upon the collective life of our biosphere. In an earlier chapter we read that the detailed study of species was known as autecology, while synecology was the investigation of actual communities. Obviously, familiarity with the structure and interrelationships of organisms and populations and their environments would be of little real aid if we did not follow this up with applied work. In other words, we should endeavour to put to good use the information that we may glean and acquire from our studies in the field. Most people's activities in everyday life fall under the heading of 'art', simply because they have not undertaken any scientific reading or training in specific natural subjects. Once, however, we pass from the arts to proper scientific bases then we are entering the realm of facts and competent definition.

DESCRIPTIONS

The first task in applied ecological field studies is to describe the subjects to be investigated. Observations and studies would be of poor quality if we could not define points of reference and so be able to check our results and compare what we see or learn with other material or previous and future work. For example, when dealing with communities, it is desirable to be able to compare those you are studying with others of similar types in different habitats. This helps in assessing any conclusions eventually reached. In applied ecology, we are dealing with a very wide variety of material and so some kind of classification and references aid our minds to grasp all the aspects of the life forms, environments and factors that are presented to us.

In some countries, notably on the continent of Europe, ecologists have constructed elaborate systems of classification. Thus in describing communities of vegetation, which farmers usually call stands of plants, the term *phytosociology* (Greek, *phyton*, plant) has been employed. We generally call natural climax vegetation types *plant formations*. Typical examples would be deciduous and coniferous forests, or grasslands or tundra. Within these major groups, many smaller, quite well-defined and variable assemblages of plants may be found, which are known as *associations* or *consociations*. These last noted can be easily recognised by the dominant species existing in each site. If there is a single dominant type, then the consociation, as it would be called, is named after it. Where there are more dominants, the association, as it will be referred to, is given a hyphened title. For instance, in a strongly growing beechwood, the beech is probably in full control and the consociation will be a beech one only; but in a mixed forest, perhaps oak and ash trees are dominant and thus that site would be an oak-ash association. Inside consociations and associations, we may find small communities of single species, such as a group of flowering bulbs on the ground or perhaps orchids on a tree branch, which may constitute small societies of their own. When communities represent stages or sequences in seres of a succession, not yet at climax point, they can be called *consocies, associes* or *socies*.

Because types of climax vegetation vary so greatly throughout the world, it is not possible to mention all the kinds that may be seen in different regions. In Great Britain, however, the chief natural climaxes are: oakwoods, beechwoods, ashwoods, and moorlands and heaths. Considerable disparity exists between areas, and there are contrasting kinds of undergrowth, secondary layers and field layers of plants.*

*Note: It should be borne in mind that in ancient times, such natural climaxes in Great Britain also contained abundant animal life. Bears, wolves, deer, wild boar, and other creatures lived in the woodlands, as part of the local ecosystems. Virtually all wild life of larger types was however, destroyed by man through hunting or official policy. The wolves and bears in England became extinct by about or soon after the twelfth century.

Having decided what type of climax we are working in, the next step would be to define the association or consocation we are dealing with. One can classify this aspect by giving individual species a frequency value, that is to say noting how often they occur in the particular locality being studied. Making up a table of frequency values may be tackled as follows:

Species	Assessment of frequency	Symbol
(Enter names	dominant	d
of types	co-dominant	co-d
observed)	very abundant	va
	abundant	a
	frequent	f
	occasional	o
	rare	r
	very rare	vr

Similar observations may be made in respect of animals, marine organisms and insects, or indeed any sorts of situations. The reader can devise tables based on the above example to cover studies of different conditions or circumstances.

SAMPLING

Various methods of taking samples are used in ecology. They should, however, be employed in conjunction with good field observations, otherwise one could become so immersed in statistics that one would lose sight of general factors. In other words, the trees would not be seen because the student or practitioner was examining the wood too closely. Here are some sampling techniques:

Line transect

This is a quick method, especially for investigating vegetation which grows on a hillside or gradient or changes due to differing water tables, salinity, or variation in soils, as well as other circumstances.

Procedure: Take a line running arbitrarily across the area to be studied, or up the gradient, and mark it with a long string, fixed on pegs. Now follow the line, writing down the species you observe growing or the habitat conditions, at fixed distances. Depending on the size of the area and the length of the

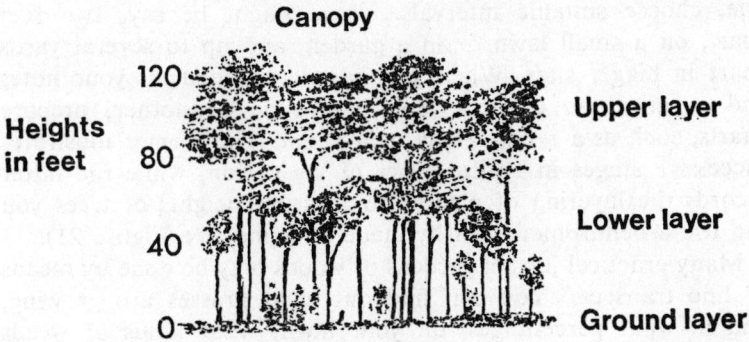

Figure 20 Example of profile chart or bisect.

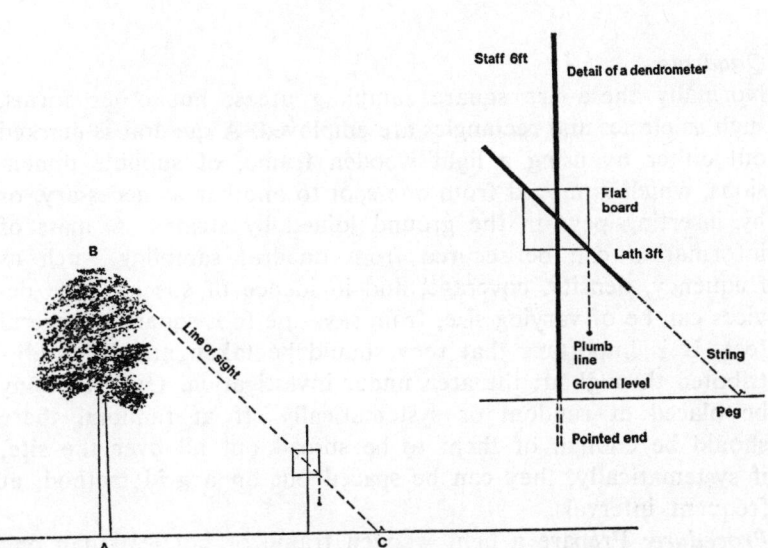

Figure 21 Using a dendrometer for measuring the height of a tree. The staff is placed at a distance from the tree, so that, with the plumb line exactly perpendicular, the diagonal lath points to the top of the tree. The person taking the sight rests on one knee to bring the eye to the lower end of the lath. The sight line is then extended to the ground by means of a string. From the point C, where this touches the ground to the centre of the trunk at the base A, will represent the actual height of the tree. The horizontal line AC is equal to the vertical AB of the triangle.

F

line, choose suitable intervals. These might be say, two feet apart, on a small lawn or in a garden, and up to several yards apart in bigger sites. When you have completed all your notes and covered the transect from one end to another, prepare charts, such as a *profile chart* or a *bisect*. The former illustrates successive stages in typical types of vegetation, while the latter records the layering of plants. To measure heights of trees you can use a dendrometer, easily made at home (see Figure 21).

Many practical jobs in gardens or woods may be done by means of line transects. You can find out what grasses are growing, and in what percentages, on your lawn; what kinds of weeds exist on your property; how you might plan the heights and densities of copses or shrubberies, and many other useful activities or improvement schemes. Should plantains or thistles be a nuisance in grassed areas, it is quick and simple to estimate their populations in this way and then calculate what quantities of weedkiller you would have to obtain to eliminate them.

Quadrats

Normally these are square sampling areas, but other forms, such as circles and rectangles are employed. A quadrat is marked out either by using a light wooden frame, of suitable dimensions, which is moved from one spot to another as necessary, or by inserting pegs in the ground joined by strings. A mass of information can be secured from quadrat sampling, such as frequency, density, coverage, and incidence of species. The devices can be of varying size, from say, one foot square to several feet. It is important that they should be taken around or distributed throughout the area under investigation. Quadrats may be placed at random or systematically. If at random, there should be enough of them to be spread out all over the site; if systematically, they can be spaced out on a grid method, at frequent intervals.

Procedure: Prepare a light wooden frame of not less than one foot square or whatever shape you may prefer, or collect a number of pegs, knock them into the ground and join them by lengths of string. The arrangement can be moved about within the area you are sampling. If it is random sampling, then ensure that you cover all sections of the site. Should you prefer systematic sampling then imagine that a grid pattern of lines is in existence over the surface of the area you are studying and starting at the base line, move your device regularly up and across the imaginary grid, taking stops at fixed intervals to do sampling. Sometimes, permanent quadrats are set out and left in position for weeks, months, or even years to observe changes. For this you will need as many frames or pegs and strings as you want devices.

The choice between random sampling and systematic sampling will depend on the nature of the site or conditions, and here the main object is to get full coverage of an area. Consequently, only the investigator can sum up adequately just which method he or she will use after looking over the place, in the light of local circumstances. Because ground or situations vary so much, the guiding principle must be to ensure that you include all the possible variables in a complex site within the scope of your sampling quadrats. A quadrat should be examined carefully and all relevant information on species, density, conditions, and other factors recorded. This is combined with similar details from other quadrats, and the whole mass of data assessed. To do this successfully, you must generally know what you are looking for, or what you want to find out, or what problem you wish to solve, otherwise much time can be wasted.

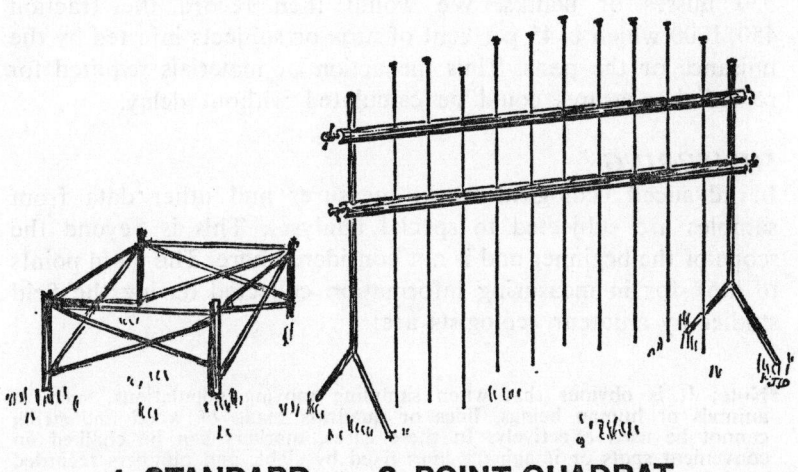

1. STANDARD   2. POINT QUADRAT

Figure 22   Quadrats.

Sometimes, belt quadrats are employed, following a transect line of the kind mentioned already.*

Point quadrats
This is a quicker method. It is valuable for discovering percentages and distribution of species in certain suitable areas.
Procedure: A frame of wood, consisting of two horizontal bars supported by two stands is prepared. Normally, about ten long thin old bicycle spokes or curtain rods, spaced two inches apart, are inserted through the bars. They should slide freely so that the device can be utilised on uneven ground. The ends of these pins, as they are called, should be sharpened, so that they will just enter the ground, as necessary. In working the point quadrat, we place the apparatus at random or systematically over an area and let down the pins in turn, seeing whether they fall on or miss species of plants or ground conditions. It is then possible to work out the percentage of species or effects present by counting the number of hits or misses. Suppose, for example, we were looking for worm casts on a lawn or caterpillars in a cabbage patch. By taking perhaps one hundred well distributed samples with the point quadrat we might find that we got, out of the 1,000 pin drops made, 450 hits on earth voided by the worms, or on grubs devouring the greenstuff, and 550 misses or blanks. We would then record the fraction 450/1000 which is 45 per cent of area or subjects infested by the nuisance or the pests. Thus the action or materials required for remedial measures could be calculated without delay.

MEASURING
In advanced ecological work, measures and other data from samples are subjected to special analyses. This is beyond the scope of the beginner and is not considered here. The main points to look for in measuring information collected during the field studies by amateur ecologists are:

---

*Note: It is obvious that when sampling moving populations, such as animals or human beings, lines or quadrats made of wood and string cannot be used effectively. In these cases, markers can be chalked on convenient spots or imaginary lines fixed by sight, and numbers recorded as they pass through or live in the sampling zones.
†Earthworms are pests only when they are in the wrong place, just as a 'weed' is a plant growing in a position disliked by man.

Lists of species

When using a sampling procedure, you can enter the information you record in graph form, plotting species against number of quadrats to make interesting and useful diagrams. In places where the curve on the graph flattens this shows that generally speaking few fresh species have been observed.

Charting

In permanent quadrats, where the changes are observed over longer periods, in detail, charts can be made of the alteration in conditions. By using different colours to show different species or occupancies by organisms of the areas studied, helpful and instructive charts can be prepared in series to illustrate how places change in course of time.

Frequency

We can express frequencies in terms of percentage of any given species or condition found in the sum total of quadrats in sampling. To define frequency classes, the following table can be used:

Frequency %	Class	Assessment
1 – 20	A	rare/occasional
21 – 40	B	frequent
41 – 60	C	abundant
61 – 80	D	very abundant
81 – 100	E	dominant

Determinations of frequency can be most helpful in applied ecology in assisting us to decide on practical questions, such as: Should we move to a new area? Would we find conditions to our liking in certain places or situations? or, what numbers of organisms would we expect to meet in different localities?

Example: in 100 quadrats a total of 2,500 specimens of a given species were recorded. The frequency percentage could be noted therefore as

$$\frac{2500}{100} = 25\%.$$ This species would be classed as frequent.

*   *   *

Edge effects

Small quadrats in sampling can lead to more errors than larger ones. This is because individual organisms which exist at the edges may or may not be included in the count, depending on the preferences of the observer. It is safest to allow an edge effect of ±10% in the final figures worked out to allow for such variations.

Cover

This refers to the areas occupied by individual species or populations and to the total of all types. Care has to be taken in estimating or calculating cover.

Performance

This may be measured in terms of yield or productivity.

TREATMENT OF INFORMATION

Quite simple and useful results may be obtained by treating data collected in elementary studies in certain ways. Generally speaking, we may wish to know more about how to compare two conditions or situations, to discover the changes that are occurring over periods of time, or to see how variations in life are related to environmental differences or alterations. It is also valuable to understand the directions or trends that will affect ecosystems, because it is these movements that bear so forcefully upon our habitats or individual niches.

An easy way of representing, in graphical manner, some or all of the above noted points is to prepare histograms. In these, the frequency distribution of organisms or events is clearly illustrated by a series of rectangles of various sizes or heights. To relate the behaviour of life forms to environmental factors we can also set out the information available in diagrams, which will show in straightforward and simple ways how situations stand or in what manner conditions may alter.

SPECIMENS

The collection of specimens is one of the most interesting parts of applied ecological studies. Using proper methods of mounting and keeping the examples of your investigations will enable you to build up a sort of reference library of great value for both

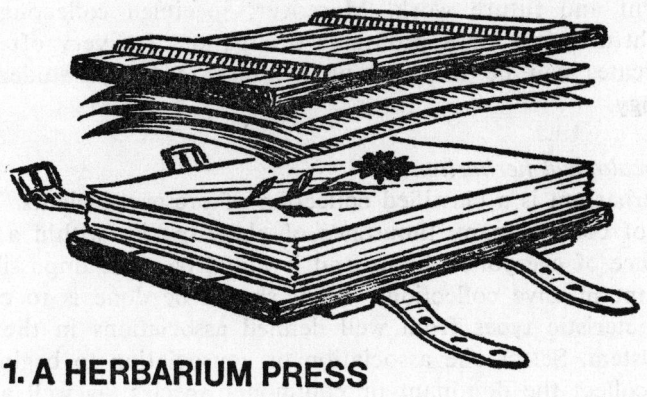

1. A HERBARIUM PRESS

2. MOUNTING SPECIMENS

Figure 23   How to prepare plants for the Herbarium.

present and future work. Moreover, specimen collecting is a delightful hobby or a profitable occupation, for very often the duplicates can be disposed of to shops or other students of ecology.

An ecological herbarium

A herbarium is a classified collection of preserved plants. There are, of course, many thousands of plant species within a short distance of everyone's home and it would be quite impossible to attempt massive collections. What should be done is to choose characteristic types from well defined associations in the local ecosystem. Select one association or consociation to begin with and collect the dominant or commoner species, as well as any species that indicate what sorts of habitats exist. Plants prefer differing conditions according to the growth patterns and food needs of the various kinds. Certain species like damp situations, others dry ones, some thrive on lime-containing soils, whilst others may flourish best in acidic ground. Horticultural books or works on agriculture, as well as standard texts on flora, generally list such preferences.

In collecting plants, the roots or rhizomes should be taken along with the aerial portions and any fruits or flowers and seeds available. Always record the place where you found the specimens, as well as the season, which layers they occupied in stratified groups or communities, and such points of interest as to whether they formed small societies of their own, occurred in relative abundance, or other useful factors. It is simplest to arrange collections of specimens to correspond with the associations from which they came. This preserves the natural continuity of living patterns. It is indeed quite possible that the same species may therefore appear repeatedly in groups of plants, but the value for the exercise of this procedure is that one can see the various local niches that they occupy, and note any differences that can arise amongst specimens of one species growing in contrasting conditions in company with other species of varying types. In technical terms, such minor disparities would represent *ecotype* variations.

Specimens should be collected in the field and placed in a vasculum or botanists collecting case, which can be bought from suppliers of equipment for naturalists. When you reach home, take out the plants carefully and lay them out on sheets of newspaper, in as normal a position as possible. Any very thick or juicy parts can be first sliced in half with a sharp knife or an old-fashioned cut-throat razor. Now, place more sheets of newspaper over the specimens and put these different newspaper-covered plants one on top of the other to form layers. The whole lot of layers is then placed in the plant press and the straps tightened carefully. Every three days, open the press, carefully remove the specimens from the paper and put them individually on fresh sheets, returning all to the press in the same manner as before.

Plant presses are simple to make. They consist of two boards of five-ply wood, measuring 10½ in. by 16½ in. each, held together by stout straps. If the straps are made of webbing canvas so much the better. The boards should have a few ¼ in. diameter holes in them to permit moisture to escape during pressing.

When the specimens are properly dry, which may take up to a month, depending on the time of year and the room they are pressed in, remove them and mount them carefully on herbarium sheets of cartridge paper, which are obtainable from good stationers or bookshops. These measure 10½ in. by 16½ in. Strips of sellotape or gummed paper can be used for mounting, fixed across specimens at suitable points to hold them gently but firmly to the paper. Herbarium papers, with affixed specimens may be placed in files and kept in cupboards, or mounted on cardboard for hanging on walls or putting in appropriate places for easy reference or viewing. Any room or shed used for herbarium purposes must be dry and clean. Moth balls or other repellents should be kept in the vicinity of the specimens to discourage attacks by insects. Painting of dried and preserved plants with a solution of mercuric chloride in alcohol will get rid of any mites or other pests that may be found on them. Mosses do not need pressing, they can be just left to dry and kept in envelopes or folded pieces of paper. You can let them soak for a short time in water whenever you want them to straighten out or swell up for examination, drying them out again afterwards.

It is very important to label all herbarium specimens carefully or confusion and muddles can result. Labels should be glued to the cartridge paper sheets next to the plants at the time they are attached to them. The label should read:

```
HERBARIUM OF ..................
Name of specimen:  ......................
Association or consociation:  .......................
Place  collected:  ........................
Date:  ....................... Layer:  .....................
Abundance:  ......... Local society or not:  .........
Habitat  factors:  ........................
Remarks:  ...............................
        ...............................
```

You can certainly use common or popular names of plants in your herbarium, or if you wish, the botanical or Latin names as well. Many useful guides to the field identification of both wild and cultivated species can be bought from bookshops, in addition to national lists of flora, which are illustrated, and contain keys for recognising vegetation.

Living collections
Excellent collections of living plants can be made quite easily. Suitable species should be dug up carefully, with some of the soil in which they are growing left around their roots, and transferred to pots, troughs or small plots of ground in the house garden or greenhouse. Proper labelling is essential and all particulars should be recorded, as for the herbarium. In this way, if desired, miniature or small replicas may be made at home of the field associations or consociations observed in nature.

Similarly, many interesting and educational zoos or collections of living animals, insects and birds or other species may be formed and their habits observed. If small organisms are kept, space should not be a problem, and the more natural the conditions that can be provided the more valuable will be the exercises. A formicarium or formicary is an ants' nest. Ants can be a source of much fascination and interest. Nests can be carefully dug out and provided a queen or some eggs are in the collection, may continue in healthy and satisfactory condition for many years after removal to the new site. To ensure that the ants do not desert the nest, place it, as unbroken and complete as possible, on a large board fitted with legs and put the whole device to stand in a flat pan or tub of water. The water should not, of course, come up over the board, but just below its edges. The ants will not pass into or attempt to cross the liquid, but will stay within the nest and the confines of the board. Adequate stocks of food and some extra building materials, such as small twigs, dry grass, and similar substances should be put near the nest from time to time, and enough earth to enable the ants to do repairs or extend the habitation as they wish to. The insects like small seeds, sugar, breadcrumbs, scraps of meat, fresh dead caterpillars, flies and other suitable edibles. A little fresh greenstuff can be given occasionally.

To secure better observation of ants you can arrange the original nesting material you collected to stand against a sheet of clear glass fastened to one side of the board on which the formicary stands. Cover this glass on the outer side with a piece of black material to exclude light. The ants will rebuild their nest with many of the internal passages and perhaps rooms visible through the glass, so by removing the covering periodically for short intervals you can see inside the nest and observe some of the insects' comings and goings. Do not, of course, forget to replace the covering after your viewing is finished, or the ants will desert the side of the nest resting against the glass, because they dislike light penetrating in the interior of the formicary for any considerable length of time. Some species of ants keep greenfly and drink their secretions, using them as the equivalent of human beings' cows, even to the extent of stroking the aphids gently to milk them. Others cultivate gardens full of small edible fungi. There is, in fact, much to observe in the social and economic life of an ant community, which may well give you a great deal of food for thought.

Apart from dogs and cats, many other small animals may be maintained satisfactorily at home and studied ecologically. It is, however, essential to remember that one should never acquire or keep any specimen that one is not prepared to look after well in proper surroundings. Ferrets, rats, mice, hamsters, cavies or guinea-pigs, bantams, rabbits, hedgehogs, land tortoises, water tortoises or terrapins, aquarium or pond fish, cage birds, such as canaries, waxbills, finches and other seedeaters, budgerigars, lovebirds and parroquets, as well as other species, will provide the observer with a wealth of information on the habits and behaviour of individual life forms. Larger animals of domestic types, including horses, cattle, sheep, pigs, goats, poultry of all kinds, and waterfowl, may often be studied on farms. Ornithology or the study of birds is most rewarding, and if you like bird watching you can, with the aid of a good pair of binoculars and handbooks on wild birds, accumulate a mass of detailed information. In some countries, observation of big game is practicable, although the numbers of such animals has greatly declined. Finally, but by no means least, study of human beings is a vital part of ecology and perhaps more important in many ways than those of other organisms. Do not, therefore, neglect to pursue assiduously the investigation of man and his society, his behaviour and the ecosystems in which he lives.

Taxidermy
This is the art of preparing, stuffing and mounting the skins of animals. It is not by any means as popular as it used to be. Taxidermy is the equivalent in animal terms to what a herbarium is for plants. It enables the student or practitioner to build up a collection of different preserved species for information and reference. Nevertheless, the process of preparation and treatment of the material is much more complicated. Readers interested should consult books on the subject.

EQUIPMENT
The beginner does not require much equipment, and certainly no expensive items, for the first steps in practical ecology. A notebook and pencil, a good lens or magnifying glass, trowel and hand fork, vasculum, knife, and a few other incidentals will suffice to start with. The materials needed for preserving specimens have already been mentioned. In addition, a camera is a great asset, because with it you can secure a pictorial record of living and environmental subjects that will be of incalculable

value for carrying out applied work. Good photographs are very important in ecology. Certain aspects of pollution, such as noise, and the behaviour of organisms, including their cries, calls, and movement sounds, as well as the speech of human beings, can be quickly and easily recorded if you possess a light tape-recorder. And a magnetic compass is also very useful to keep check on direction in the field.

For more advanced studies, extra equipment will be necessary. Some of this may be required for investigation of aquatic environments, while other items are needed for terrestrial exercises. To keep records of climatic conditions, you will have to set up a rain-gauge or pluviometer, maximum and minimum thermometers for ascertaining temperatures and their fluctuations, and wet and dry bulbs for recording relative humidity. Meteorological equipment is usually housed in a Stevenson pattern screen. This is a white box standing on legs, with a sloping roof and double louvred walls. The external dimensions are normally about 26 in. by 23 in. by 16½ in. deep. Other useful requisites include sunshine recorders, wind vanes, air pollution samplers, barometers, and anemometers, the last named being used for measuring winds. All these instruments can be purchased from suppliers of scientific apparatus with full instructions for their use.*

Ecologists employ more elaborate apparatus for specialised field investigations, and although these do not really concern the beginner, it is of interest to mention some of the items concerned and to discuss later one or two of the tests that can be carried out with them. Here is a short list:

Item	Purpose
Aquatic and plankton nets	for catching samples of fish and plankton
Water sampler	taking specimens of water
Dissolved oxygen meter	measures oxygen in solution in natural waters
Water conductivity meter	water purity measurement

*For example, Baird & Tatlock Ltd., Freshwater Road, Chadwell Heath, Essex, England, and in the United States, ...

Dark and light bottles	measuring oxygen changes in water
Bottom grabs	taking up mud from pond or lake bottoms
Sieves	screening
Filters	filtering
Centrifuge	centrifuging (rapid rotation to separate substances of different densities)
Weighing scales	weighing specimens and materials
Spectrophotometer	combines functions of a spectroscope and a photometer
Mammal traps	catching mammals painlessly
Respirometer	measuring respiration
Soil sampler	taking soil samples
Manometer	measures pressures of gases
Soil tensiometer	measures capillary potential of soil
Microscope	magnification
Thermistor	measures soil temperatures
Photometer and exposuremeter	measure light intensities
Atmometer	measures evaporating power of the air or rate of evaporation from a moist surface
Potometer	measures transpiration rates
Colorimeters	comparators and colour discs for assessing alkalinity and acidity

Sampling a Lake or Pond
Some of the above noted equipment would be used in more advanced sampling of lakes or ponds. The water sampler can extract a column of water at any desired depth. Part of this water would then be centrifuged to concentrate the phytoplankton for counting under a microscope, while another portion would be filtered to remove all microorganisms. When the second lot is placed in acetone, the chlorophyll and other pigments are extracted, giving a clear green solution which when put in a spectrophotometer will reveal the actual quantities of these materials that it contains. The amount of chlorophyll in a pond or lake will be a good indicator of the food making potential at any time because it increases or decreases as photosynthesis varies, adjusting to light, temperature and available nutrients. By using a plankton net, which is made from very fine mesh silk or nylon, and drawing it through the water, zooplankton may be sampled. A seine or fish net will catch species of fish, while a bottom grab can bring up mud and sediment from the bottom of the lake or pond to analyse. It is possible therefore, employing these tools or apparatus, to obtain a clear picture of the producers and consumers living in the water under investigation, as far as number, types, biomass, and chlorophyll are concerned. So an ecologist could build up an understanding of how pond or lake function and what sort of yield, in fishing terms, could be expected from it.

Dark and light bottle tests
The purpose of these tests is to measure oxygen changes in water resulting from plankton metabolism, that is chemical changes produced by these organisms. Sets of bottles of dark and light colour are prepared, by covering some with black tape or aluminium foil and leaving others without any cover. Pairs of light and dark bottles, containing samples of water from each of several levels in a pond or lake, are now suspended at the same depths from which the water was drawn. After twenty-four hours, they are removed and the oxygen in each fixed by manganous sulphate, alkaline iodide, and sulphuric acid reagents. This treatment causes a colour change to brown in the water in the bottles by effecting release of elemental iodine. The darker the brown colour, the more oxygen there will be in the water

samples. By adding sodium thiosulphate until the colour disappears, and noting the volume used in each case, the concentration of oxygen can be calculated. The decline in oxygen in the dark bottles indicates the amount of respiration in the water column, whereas the oxygen changes in the light bottles show the net photosynthesis. The two quantities added together give an estimate of total food production by the organisms.

STATISTICS

The statistical treatment of ecological data is not within the scope of this book and the beginner will not be concerned with the details, but because statistics affect all of us so much in this present age, as well as for the benefit of any reader who may later wish to undertake more advanced study in applied ecology, a brief mention is made here of the general ways in which statistical analyses can be of help in environmental biology.

Much of the material that we obtain in ecological field investigations concerns the density and frequency of occurrences of organisms, together with details about individual species.

When we come to compare sampling results, it is possible to judge if any difference between them and normal distribution curves are true ones or have been caused by chance arising from sampling of variable material.

Readers interested in the application of statistical methods in ecological work can obtain detailed information on their use and how to employ calculation techniques, in books on statistics, such as:

Statistical Methods, G. W. Snedecor, Iowa State College Press, Ames, Iowa, U.S.A.;
Statistical Analysis in Biology, K. Mather, Methuen & Co., Ltd., London; or
Statistical Tables for Biological, Agricultural & Medical Research, R. A. Fisher & F. Yates, Oliver & Boyd, Edinburgh.

EXERCISES

Many kinds of simple exercises in applied ecoolgy can be undertaken at home or in the field, which will add much interest and enrichment to the reader's studies. Apart from their value in adding to general practical knowledge of the science, such activities can be an interesting hobby or often turn out to be profitable and contribute to well-being and happiness.

Here are a few suggestions for some easily carried out ecological exercises. No doubt readers will be able to think of many more similar ones designed to take advantage of local conditions and circumstances, or which may solve problems and abate nuisances.

(1) A pest is decimating the plants in your garden. Conduct an ecological assessment of the situation, and on the basis of the results suggest remedies including any possible biological controls.

(2) You are worried by the appearance of what seem to you to be a large number of tramps in your neighbourhood. Carry out a survey by quadrat sampling to discover if your fears are really justified.

(3) You have heard mice or rats moving about your premises at night. Trap and mark a number of the animals, then release them and re-trap a quantity to find out the probable total population of the intruders.

(4) A nearby river or lake, which formerly held a good stock of fish, is now useless for angling. Survey the watercourse or site and after investigations endeavour to locate the cause of the changed circumstances.

(5) Certain attractive species of wild birds use to nest and live periodically around your house and garden. Now they no longer do so. Undertake a study of the matter and see if you can identify any probable reasons for the disappearance of the birds.

(6) A member of your family is behaving in a peculiar way. Conduct an ecological observation of the conduct in question and relate the facts to possible causes.

(7) In a wood near your home, tree seedlings are being seriously damaged. Ascertain what organisms are responsible and why they are able to carry out these depredations.

(8) A field belonging to a farmer is full of thistles, but the grass is always quite short. Why is it so infested with these weeds?

(9) In a nearby beechwood there are hardly any shrubs or ground layer plants, but in an adjacent stand of ashes there are large numbers of smaller species growing prolifically under the big trees. What is the main reason for this difference?

(10) Hamsters quarrel when placed together in confinement, but cavies or guinea-pigs may live together quite happily. Why is this?

(11) Why are hill and mountain areas in the British Isles virtually devoid of forests today, and what would you expect to find if you examined the heaths and moorlands in such districts?

(12) When studying a river flowing through farm fields used for growing cereal crops what would you be most likely to observe in the water and why would it be there?

(13) Why are there so few insects in industrial towns?

(14) Fungus diseases spread most rapidly through agricultural or garden crops. What do you think is the chief cause of this problem?

(15) Dogs are generally kindly looked after and well fed in some countries but often rather cruelly treated and ill-nourished in others. Could you give any important reason for this difference?

(16) Many farmers uproot hedgerows today to make very large fields. What effects does this action have on the countryside?

(17) One kind of litter is far worse than other sorts. Do you know what it is and why it is so objectionable?

(18) Give a reason why a newly built dam may become useless after some years.

(19) Why do you think the destruction of forests leads to development of barren and desert conditions?

(20) Excessive industrialisation causes a drain on one of the essentials of life. What is it?

(21) Name some signs of air pollution.

(22) Discuss how soil erosion affects food supplies.

(23) Why are refuse dumps objectionable?

(24) What damage does increased use of pesticides do?

(25) Is it dangerous to dump waste materials into seas and inland waters?

(26) Which is more important for man's future – the environment or economic and industrial growth?

(27) Discuss some ways of becoming more self-sufficient.

(28) Mention some of the ways in which man has upset the balance of nature.

(29) What effect may the destruction of vegetation have on the atmosphere?

(30) Why is rain water often harmful to health in many areas?

(31) List some environmental factors of your locality.

(32) Do you know what kind of ecosystem you are living in?

(33) What is your niche in your habitat?

(34) What signs of aggression are apparent in your community?

(35) What stage in the succession pattern do you think your society has reached? Is it progressing, static or declining?

(36) If the sere you are in now is not at climax what do you consider would be a satisfactory one?

(37) What imbalances do you notice in your ecosystem?

(38) What are the limiting factors in your surroundings?

(39) What biotic influences exert pressure on the local environment?

(40) How does your community tolerate natural or man-made conditions and what adaptations has it made to cope with its habitat?

(41) List your present conditions of life on an ecological assessment form, noting environmental, climatic and biotic factors and influences that limit your progress.

(42) State some personal or business problems and assess them in ecological terms.

(43) Are you satisfied with your present habitat? If not, how can you improve it?

(44) Do you like your present niche? If not, have you any plans to change it?

(45) Can you tolerate your existing conditions? If not, could you make a move to better ones?

(46) Do aggression and competition from other individuals affect you and are you successful or unsuccessful in combating them?

(47) Could ecology help you to live harmoniously, by (a) helping you to understand life and nature better, and (b) showing you how to deal with problems and difficulties in many cases?

(48) What adaptations are you conscious of having made in your life recently?

(49) Would you be willing to set aside up to half-an-hour daily to think over your affairs in ecological terms?

(50) Write down a list of all the things you really want to do and assess each item for its practicability in relation to its possible achievement through applied ecology.

Answers and comments on exercises

To assist the reader in going through the exercises set out above, some brief answers, where these would be appropriate, and comments, are given below. Many of the queries listed, however, demand replies which will be specific in nature and peculiar to individual circumstances, so it is not practicable here to respond to them generally. In fact, the answers in these cases should be found by conscientious study of all relevant material assembled through ecological assessment of situations or questions.

(1) Use a process of elimination to arrive at the solution. Find out what organism is predatory on the pest.

(2) Refer to frequency table* to see if number noticed is really low or high, and if your fears were justified, after you have done the sampling and counting.

*See page 165.

(3) This is a population census by the marking method.

(4) The cause is probably pollution or poisoning by industrial waste from factories.

(5) Biotic factors or man-made influences may be responsible.

(6) This demands a thorough ecological assessment of all the circumstances.

(7) Possibly mice or voles are destroying the seedlings because the natural predators of these animals have been killed by human activities.

(8) Overgrazing of the grass by livestock has eliminated competition for the thistles and allowed them to grow freely.

(9) Beech trees suppress other species because of the dense canopy they form, whereas ashes form more open upper layers, thus admitting sufficient light for secondary and ground layers of vegetation to exist fairly easily.

(10) Hamsters, in nature, live separately except for very short periods at mating time, whereas cavies are normally found in groups.

(11) In early times, the British hill areas were clothed in forests. Man destroyed these over the centuries, and the ground, after the removal of the tree cover, suffered intensified leaching, so that today it is too acid or waterlogged to support woodlands.

(12) Excessive algae formation or greening of the water, caused by effluents produced by quantities of ill-balanced fertilisers draining from the fields.

(13) The cause is serious air pollution.

(14) Monoculture, where large stands of single species encourage rapid spread of diseases. In nature, the species are mixed.

(15) Dogs, like other carnivorous animals, compete with human beings for scarce food supplies. In affluent countries this is no problem, but in poor lands there would not be enough nourishment to go around, so the dogs are deprived.

(16) Erosion of the soil by wind action and destruction of beneficial wild life and insects.

(17) Plastics, because they do not break down naturally.

(18) Silting up, due to failure to conserve watersheds.

(19) When there is no vegetation present the soil loses moisture. Solar energy is re-radiated and lost. The land dries up and rainfall diminishes. Erosion completes the destruction and serious dessication sets in.

(20) Water. Industrial societies consume vast quantities of water and this loss causes lowering of water tables.

(21) Destruction of vegetation and wild life, smog, oxygen shortage in cities, effects on lichens and mosses, as well as other influences.

(22) Ruins land for farming.

(23) Diseases can spread from dumps to surrounding areas.

(24) Apart from destroying beneficial animals and insects, pesticides can enter the food chain.

(25) This practice causes pollution and poisoning of fishes, birds and other marine or fresh water life and of the waters themselves.

(26) Give your views.

(27) Consider some self-sustaining communities.

(28) Discuss pollution, land damage, extermination of species and other activities.

(29) Eventually a diminution in oxygen content.

(30) It may contain lead and other poisons in industrial areas.

(31) Consider all the various factors bearing on the ecology of the locality.

(32) Describe the type of ecosystem.

(33) State your way of making a living, status and other circumstances.

(34) List these behaviour patterns.

(35) Define it, with reasons for your conclusions. If static, say if this is a climax.

(36) Explain what climax you feel would be a good and balanced one.

(37) List the imbalances.

(38) Describe the factors involved.

(39) Record all these influences.

(40) Explain toleration and any adaptations made to allow for conditions.

(41) Complete the form given in this book or prepare one for yourself.

(42) Use a suitably modified form to express problems fully.

(43) Discuss all aspects of position.

(44) Similar response as in (43).

(45) Examine position in detail.

(46) Review these aspects and evaluate your responses. If you are unsuccessful, see how you might improve your performance.

(47) Think over all the possibilities of using applied ecology in your life.

(48) Evaluate any adaptations made.

(49) Time spent in this way could result in more efficiency in daily activities.

(50) A review of hopes and ambitions, if they are practicable, and how you might achieve them is, in itself, an exercise in self-confidence.

These answers and comments are necessarily rather cursory, but are intended to serve only as guidelines. The reader should greatly expand his or her responses to the exercises. In this way, many new angles and inspirations may present themselves and serious assessment will often produce applied ecological solutions and decisions of great value and significance.

CHAPTER TEN

Ecology in Society

Many common patterns of behaviour and development can be observed in all types of organisms. The needs for food, shelter and territory, as well as the fact that each species or population is compelled to live within the limits imposed by the special environments of their particular ecosystems, which in turn must conform to the general conditions of our planet's biosphere, control and regulate the boundaries of existence on Earth. The more advanced organisms may be the more complicated and intricate will be their communal and social organisations. Man is not, of course, the only social animal. We can observe rudimentary and often quite involved patterns of simple group and herd conduct in wolves, beavers, elephants, marine mammals, cattle, deer, and numerous other animals, as well as in flocks of birds. Amongst the insects, the examples of ants, termites and bees stand out. Very many ecological studies have been undertaken of the behaviour and responses of these life forms.

EARLY MEN
Mankind's rise from primitive conditions to a position of dominance on Earth was a slow and laborious climb. In terms of scientific classification, human beings are primates, belonging to the sub-order *Anthropoidea,* which includes also the apes and monkeys. Both men and apes are grouped together in the superfamily *Hominoidea,* which is subdivided into two sections – the *Pongidae* or anthropoid apes, and the *Hominoidea,* comprising all extinct and modern types of men. As far as anatomy is concerned, the chief differences between these families is that the hominids walk erect or upright, while the pongids depend on their arms as well for locomotion at various times. The common ancestral stock of apes and men is stated to be represented by the life form *Proconsul,* which existed about twenty million

184

years ago, and which showed certain characteristics of the hominoid line which are not present in modern great apes. Pongids are specialised for life in forests. When man's forebears ventured out from the woodlands into the open plains, the arms no longer had to be employed in swinging from tree to tree and so the pelvic girdle and the lower limbs gradually became adapted to and modified for maintaining an erect position – better suited to a grassland or savannah type of existence. Moreover, this change of posture freed the hands of *Proconsul's* descendants for making and using simple tools.

The progress of the hominoids has been traced step by step through prehistory, as follows:

1. *Australopithecines:* Ape-like in appearance, but the shape of their pelvis and limb bones indicates that they had adopted the erect posture. Possibly of two species, one small and unspecialised and the other larger and more like modern gorillas. The brain was small, but bigger in relation to body size than those of present-day apes. *Australopithecus bosiei* had a huge palate with enormous molars, and was said to have lived 1,700,000 years ago and is popularly termed 'Nutcracker Man'.

2. *Homo habilis:* A more advanced hominoid, possibly a maker of stone tools.

3. *Pithecanthropus or Homo erectus:* Brain larger than in *Australopithecines,* but still small when compared with modern man. Extremely thick skull, with low and sloping forehead, very heavy brow-ridges and receding chin. The 'Erect Ape Man' was *Pithecanthropus erectus,* with a rather earlier stage known as *P. robustus,* and a sub-species called *Sinanthropus pekinensis. H. erectus* made stone and bone tools generally and no doubt used fire. As time progressed, the species evolved further and the brain became bigger. However, the forehead remained sloping and the brow-ridges well marked.

4. *Neandertaloids:* Rather brutal appearance, with heavy brow-ridges, sloping foreheads and receding chins. Often cave dwellers and buried their dead in such places. Rhodesian Man also had very large brow-ridges with a continuous bar above the eye sockets. Became extinct about 40,000 B.C.

5. *Homo sapiens:* Men of completely modern appearance probably replaced the Neandertaloids about 30,000 B.C. Cro-Magnon men possessed long heads, very large brain cases and short broad

faces and were rather tall. They were associated with the Aurigna-
cian culture, which died out about 18,000 B.C., and was followed by the Solutrian and then the Magdalenian. *Homo sapiens*
was originally a hunter, but agricultural settlements were in
being by 8000 B.C., and led to development of weaving, metal-
lurgy and wheeled vehicles.

It would appear that man's progress on Earth has been aided
by two main factors: his intelligence, which grew as his brain
size increased, and his abilities as a tool maker. The first tools
were prepared from stones and bones; then followed the use of
metals, such as copper, silver and gold and mixtures of copper
and tin or bronze. Iron, which was tougher and stronger than
bronze, gave its users an advantage in war and in the making
of utensils and implements. Nevertheless, progress has not been
equally spread over the world, due to the very different environments in which groups of men have found themselves placed.

ENVIRONMENT AND CULTURE

Most scientists are agreed that there are no significant differences
in intelligence existing between any of the various races of men
living in the world today, although there are, of course, marked
contrasts between individuals as far as intellectual ability is
concerned. Some peoples are still relatively backward because they
have lacked in their areas the raw materials or skills necessary for
general and technological advances, or as the result of historical
patterns they have remained isolated and outside the main flow
of civilisation, so that new ideas did not reach them. Environmental factors, as we know, play a very important part in the
development of any society, whether it be one of plants, animals
or men.

In human terms, a society is often described as a group of
people who live and work together. The behaviour and way of
life of such an assemblage are called a culture. We do not in
scientific language refer to the conduct of animals, insects and
birds in their social relationships or to the interactions of plants
with one another, as cultures. This is because culture, in its
human sense, indicates a kind of civilisation based on intelligence,
and is considered to cover customs, laws, religion, art, technology,
and household goods. Culture may be seen in both its material
attributes and in its intellectual spheres. Yet it is wrong to hive

off all culture entirely as a human possession. Many animals make dwelling places, store their food, organise their social lives and have primitive *mores*. Moreover, do not ants cultivate farms, keep slaves, 'milk' their herds of greenfly 'cows', and practice division of labour? It is salutory for man to remember his origins and the fact that he shares the earth with numerous other species, which have evolved in many cases very useful and ingenious ways of living. The human body does, of course, contain vestigial structures, such as a small appendix and traces of a third eyelid, as evidence of evolution, while gills such as those of fishes are formed during the early stages of mammalian development, although they disappear later.

Within major cultures a number of subcultures may be detected. Individuals may be members of more than one subculture, retaining of course their positions in the whole group culture. Societies are not always synonymous with any single culture, because they may contain several sub-cultures or ways of life. The cultures or subcultures impose behaviour patterns and customs upon the people who belong to them. Thus individuals are never really free agents, but are governed from birth to death by the rules and requirements of the culture or subculture of which they constitute parts. All social animals, including man, possess approved codes of conduct, transgressions of which incur the displeasure and objections of their fellows. Punishments administered by societies on individuals or groups that violate the written and unwritten codes, tribal habits, taboos and similar inhibitory practices are very wide ranging and may take the forms of death, expulsion, confinement, ostracism, and many further types of sanctions or pressures. Nevertheless, within most societies, competition for power, materials and better conditions is fierce between individuals, families and sectional groups. Opposed to this drive or impetus is the need for the organisms in the assemblage to cooperate together to achieve and maintain some common aims and keep the whole structure in balance. These two forces – competition and cooperation – continually pull individuals living together in contrary directions and are responsible for many of the tensions that plague social life.

Group influences impose themselves upon sectional outlooks. This banding together of major communities and populations is a relic of ancient times, but perhaps necessary in our day as well. Our forefathers were faced with an untamed natural environment, full of many hazards, with plagues, famines, frequent attacks by enemies, and wild beasts constantly prowling the forests and plains. They had few tools or facilities with which to battle with nature, nor did they possess the knowledge that we have acquired today to enable them to understand or control the conditions or surroundings in which they existed. Consequently, the only protection that they could provide for themselves was to stay in groups in order to defend their lives and property or territory against assaults from any quarter.

Modern man has modified world environments greatly and improved the health, longevity, nutrition and general living patterns of his species. But, as we know, nature is not fooled. The synthetic and artificial ecosystems that we live in have given rise to serious problems, a lot of which were unfamiliar to our ancestors. Such difficulties are generally of contemporary origin. Simpler and more natural cultures were developed as ways of life suited to particular groups with long histories of certain experiences, and adapted to specific physical environments. Modern western culture is not old; it is too broad and oppressive to suit all the individuals in any community; and it is not in harmony with any natural environment. New inventions initiate technological changes, followed by rapid cultural movements which are simply attempts to adjust to successive man-made environments with material backgrounds and fast-altering conditions. We can follow the development from technical change to shifts in societies' habits by observing, how the material invention or discovery alters economic and social structures, the effects of which changes permeate through all parts of the groups or populations involved and finally turn upside-down the general cultural attitudes.

Man, of course, does not live by bread alone, but it is very important to him and he obtains it by working. Work is performed by all organisms in their daily or nightly rounds of activity in the ceaseless search for food and shelter, as well as in reproduction and self-defence. But human beings work for more than basic essentials; they are never satisfied and desire luxuries. Nevertheless, research investigations undertaken into the nature of industrial labour have shown that work is very closely interlinked with the other factors that form and condition cultures and social patterns. Particularly notable were the conclusions that work is a social activity in the sense that what is done is carried out in or for society; that the social rounds of most adults are primarily formed around work activity; and that needs for recognition, security and a sense of belonging were more important in determining workers' morale than the physical conditions of the workplaces. In addition, status at work and feelings of individual self-respect were found to be more significant in some ways than wages, while a worker's attitudes and effectiveness at jobs were conditioned greatly by social demands both within and outside the place of work. Finally, changes in general life from static to mobile societies in an altering world environment tended to disrupt the social organisation in industries continually and create complex problems.

It must be noted, that amongst twentieth-century human beings, group collaboration does not occur normally by accident or even by force of circumstances, but has to be planned for and developed carefully. The functional and mass societies of today find it difficult to achieve cohesion, but without that attribute, it becomes increasingly hard to resist the disrupting effects of synthetic man-made environments. It has been argued that there are three types of human beings – and similar views could be taken of behaviour patterns amongst the higher animals – that rebel against society and so reflect the conflicts latent in whole communities: the neurotic, the criminal and the genius. Such specific selection of types, however, would appear to be based more on emotionalism than science. The ecological assessment would prefer to consider all the different factors that bear upon individual organisms and to work out the exact places of any rebellious ones in the succession pattern. It may well be that some of them are occupying stages ahead of (or perhaps behind) their fellows in the particular sere in question, for we all know that what may be frowned upon today might have been the fashion yesterday and could be the accepted thing tomorrow. So a rebel can be next decade's 'good boy', or might have been a hero in another age. As we have pointed out already in an earlier chapter of this book, there are few good guys or bad guys in nature.

CHAPTER ELEVEN

Self-Sufficiency and Eco-Units

The term 'self-sufficiency' is in some ways a misnomer, because as we know it is not possible for any organism to attain this status completely. All life forms are in states of dependence one upon another in greater or lesser degrees. What we therefore really mean by self-sufficiency is a reasonable condition or position of self-support. Nevertheless, as the expression 'self-sufficiency' has come to infer in popular fashion a state where individuals or communities can hope to look after themselves and survive without much outside aid, except what is provided naturally, it has been used here.

Public interest in self-sufficiency continues to grow because of several reasons. There is a marked dislike in many circles of the monolithic and interfering societies, personified in the governments and bureaucracies of our times, that seek to control and regulate the lives of people. Existence in industrial communities leads to loss of identity at the individual and family level, exposure to mass media and indoctrination campaigns, and feelings of helplessness as the racing tides of change and conditioning attempt to mould and swallow up everyone into similar patterns. Conformity is expected in social affairs and at work. Those who wish to think for themselves or 'opt out' of the way of life of the majority in groups and populations are regarded as neurotic, criminal or eccentric. Furthermore, work has often become monotonous and without any real purpose, other than a ceaseless round of boring activity, designed to pursue some elusive goal of 'growth' for purely material objectives. It is therefore small wonder that such large numbers of persons are inclined to think that participation in this sort of existence is a mere 'paper life', without any contact with nature or reality. Indeed, this may be so, for they are asked to labour for increasingly worthless payment in paper, producing often unnecessary and frivolous goods which are sold for more paper, and from birth to death they will be harassed and surrounded on all sides by more of this commodity wielded and controlled by faceless bureaucrats ensconced remotely in the well-guarded citadels of government. While, in some ways, this may perhaps be an unfair judgement of the civilisations of today, yet it is not difficult to understand such views are becoming increasingly held by so many individuals in industrial societies at the present time, nor why the search for alternative styles of living is active and forceful.

ALTERNATIVE TECHNOLOGY

In modern terms, a wide range of activity is covered by the expression alternative technology. Various schemes, including harnessing of the sun's energy, use of winds and tides and other natural forces, and many more ideas have been proposed. The impetus behind the majority of such projects can be found in younger and technically-based individuals and groups of workers, frequently in conflict with official and commercial ways of doing things. Consequently, we find that emphasis is being laid by such people or organisations primarily upon the employment and improvement of alternative sources of energy, instead of depending on non-renewable fuels. Secondly, there has been a considerable amount of effort put into the construction of life-support gardens, nature homes, and self-sustaining units for families and communities. It is believed that it should be practicable for families to be equipped to exist largely on their own resources, producing their own food and needing the minimum of servicing from outside. Such units could be grouped within easy reach of one another and provide meaningful and satisfying living patterns. Power might be obtained chiefly from modern small windmills or other devices, local materials could be utilised for building the home and for clothing the family, while the individual complexes would be fitted to conserve natural resources.

Energy can be produced from solar heat collectors, waterwheels, windmills, tidal generators and compost heaps, to mention only some of the possible devices available for the purpose, instead of relying upon coal, oil or atomic power. The basic links between all these alternative methods are conservation of resources, recycling of waste, and minimum disruption of the environment. New methane gas producing plants have been designed, which can utilise farm waste, slurries of water and dung and organic refuse in an anaerobic digestion process, to decompose the materials and produce the gas by-product. Such waste-derived gas has the same energy value as sea gas or natural gas and can be utilised as fuel for small power stations, and to drive gas engines or for vehicles. Heating, lighting, power and fuel can thus be available on farms or other premises by converting waste manures in organic gas digesters on the sites where the gas is required. The author of this book has used methane gas produced from decomposed animal dung and plant material to provide power for numerous purposes at low cost with simply made equipment, built locally, in isolated areas. A demonstration unit which generates more than 300,000 British thermal units of gas daily, employing the waste from one hundred pigs, has been constructed in the United Kingdom. It is practicable to store surplus methane gas.

Another device for energy production is flywheel storage. Such a machine might consist of a wheel or disc fifteen feet in diameter and weighing about two hundred tons. New materials such as fused silica and carbon fibres, when used for flywheels, would make it possible for the device to retain up to ten thousand kilowatt hours of energy stored in the wheel, after it had been rotated for a period. To set the flywheel spinning, the machine works as a motor, and when the energy stored in the wheel is required then the machine is reversed to become a generator, thus releasing the energy for use. All the apparatus could be concentrated into a cell about twenty feet square.

Solar stills have been built in many areas of the world. Often, however, they are bulky and use heavy materials, such as concrete, in their construction. Simpler devices, such as the Porteous still, can be made at lower cost. This particular model consists basically of four glass-roofed shallow water tanks, 49 ft. long by 10 ft. wide, made of corrosion-resistant aluminium, each held in a frame of steel girders and angle-iron supports. The tanks are lined with butyl rubber sheeting and fitted with gently sloping glass roofs. Salt water is run into the tanks and sunshine evaporates fresh water from this brine, leaving the salt behind. The vapour condenses on the underside of the glass roof and the pure water then drips into a gutter and is led away to storage

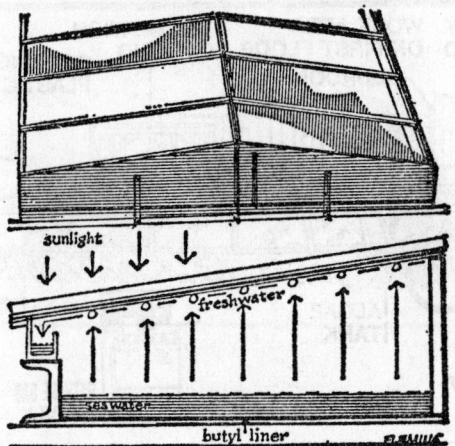

Figure 24   DESIGN OF A PORTEOUS SOLAR STILL for producing fresh water from sea or salt water.

tanks. It is necessary to renew the water supply for the still every two days, from the sea or other saline source. This takes only about five minutes to do. Such solar stills are excellent for producing constant supplies of potable water in places where there is adequate sunlight, and the local stocks of water are not usable in their natural state owing to excessive salinity.

Solar heating for domestic purposes has also been successful in many areas. Sunlight is trapped on suitable dark walls and the heat stored and utilised for various tasks. The provision of glass screens or covers a foot or more away from the front of the wall will ensure effective trapping of warmth. In regions where sunshine is intermittent, the functioning of solar heaters is naturally less efficient, but if supplemented with windmills to produce power to fill the gaps when the heat traps are not functioning fully, permanent supplies of warmth and hot water may normally be secured.

Self-sustaining houses or ecological houses, based upon contracted peasant holdings of former times, but set in industrial areas, have been designed by several interested individuals and organisations. One notable example produced in London,* was intended to make its occupants as self-sufficient as possible for heating and cooking fuels, sewage disposal, water supply and

*By Mr Graham Caine.

G

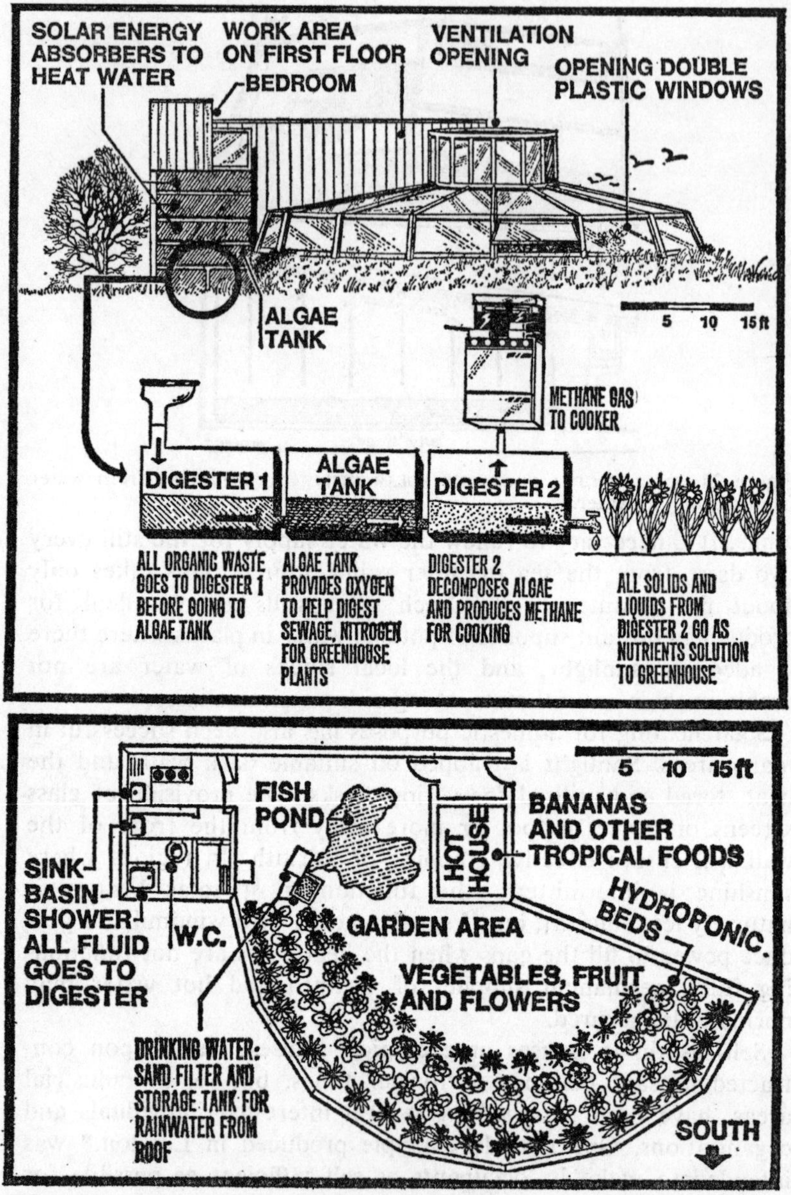

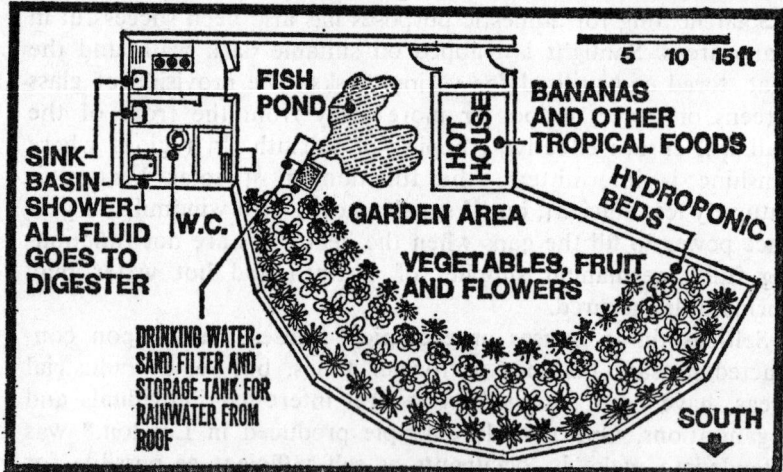

Figure 25 DESIGN FOR AN ECOLOGICAL HOUSE. (1) Side View. The enlarged detail shows the three-stage sewage recycling plant which fits under the living quarters and provides nutrients for the garden.
(2) Plan view.

foodstuffs. The house incorporated waste recycling, use of sun power, rain collecting and horticultural systems, and even a plant for brewing beer. The object of such dwellings are to reduce pollution and the consumption of natural resources, as well as to make it unnecessary to rely on centralised technical services. People living in ecological houses would run most of their own affairs. The plans for the unit in question included a sewage digestion plant which would take all liquid and solid organic wastes and produce methane gas for cooking and lighting. This digester could also give a flow of liquid nutrients for a greenhouse where vegetables and some fruits could be grown by hydroponics or soilless culture. Sunlit or illuminated tanks containing algae can kill off any disease organisms in the sewage. The algae also take up oxygen from the air to aid bacteria to digest the sewage, and nitrogen to enrich the fertiliser solution for the greenhouse plants. Five hundred square feet of warmed greenhouse in cool temperate climatic conditions should be adequate to supply a family's green-food needs, all the year around, if intensively cropped and carefully planted. The central dome of this design of house would collect warm air. On the south wall a series of blackened central-heating radiators would trap solar heat. Even on a January day in England, solar energy could warm a tank of water up to 26° C, when it was connected to these heaters, and in April a water temperature of 60°C was obtained. For winter conditions, a wind generator and power storage system would supplement the solar heating. Washing and drinking water may be collected on the roof – this is a common practice in many areas of the world – and stored for use as needed.

SELF-CONTAINED SPACECRAFT

Future spacecraft intended for long journeys to planets, and even further, perhaps outside our solar system, could be considered as eco-units or indeed small independent artificial ecosystems of their own. Similar comments might apply to Lunar or Martian colonies started to accommodate settlers from Earth. Self-contained spacecraft or settlements would have to include all the four basic components of ecosystems, that is to say, producers, consumers, decomposers and abiotic substances, in proper proportions and adequate diversity to ensure and keep stable environments able to adjust to the incoming solar radiation, just as

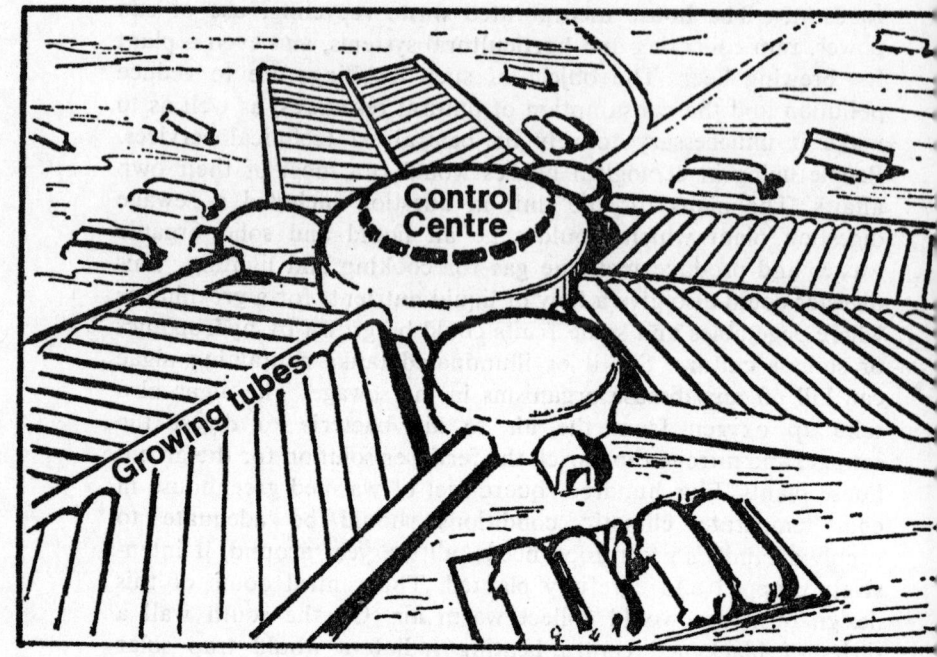

Figure 26 How an ecological production unit for growing Hydroponic crops could look like in future space settlements.

Earthly ecosystems do. Considerable research on the design and fittings of space vehicles intended to function for long periods as self-sustaining units has been commenced in the United States. Plants have been grown in controlled environments and produced large crops very rapidly. Plans have also been drawn up for the building of space colonies with food-producing farms and vegetation inside them. These installations would employ waste recycling systems, solar energy for power, and many other devices intended to make them independent of external sources, where those did not exist in useful or economic quantities.

LIFE-SUPPORT TECHNIQUES
Life-support techniques, often popularly called eco-unit systems, have attracted much attention in recent years. The ecological house design already discussed is one example of a possible installation, but there are of course numerous other construc-

tions that could be utilised for self-support in greater or lesser degrees. At the bottom of all this activity there lies a desire to return to the independent and more natural life of our rural ancestors and so break out of the restrictive straightjacket of modern industrial existence. The following notes were prepared by John Wood and Associates of Manchester and cover the field of eco-units in outline. They are reproduced here because they include a large number of points of interest that may serve to present useful ideas to readers desirous of studying or making different forms of eco-units or availing themselves of some of the methods of alternative technology.

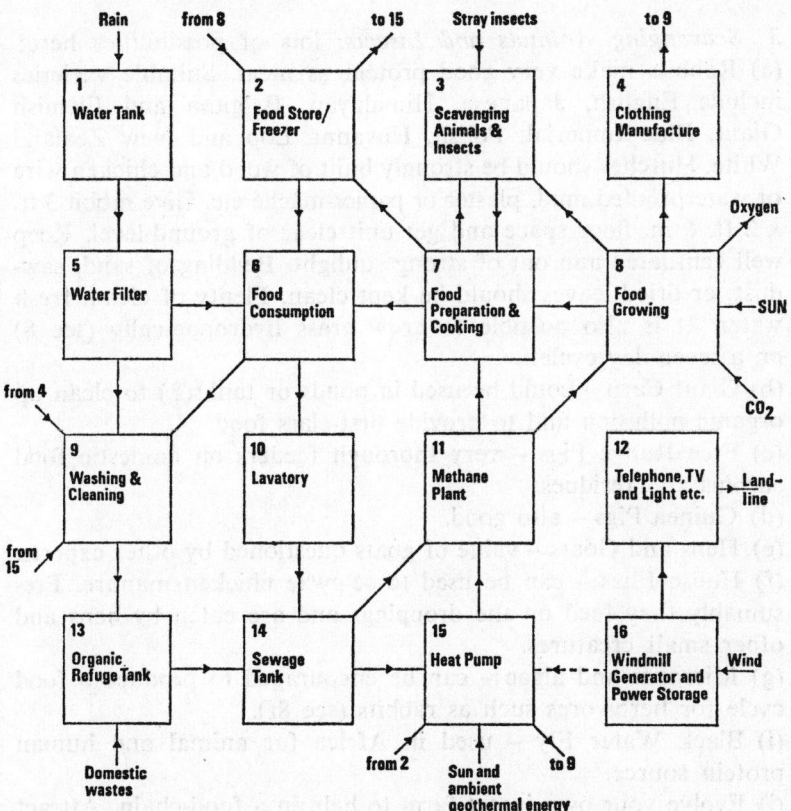

Figure 27 Key to diagrammatic representation of salient points of eco-unit systems.

Key to diagrammatic representation of salient points of eco-unit systems

1   *Water Tank:* anything from the traditional wooden barrel to re-inforced tea-chest lined with polythene. Your own idea is probably the best one.

2   *Food-Store/Freezer:* this could be part of a carefully designed heat-pump (see 15) which would transfer heat from the food-store to other parts of the system such as heaters.

Alternatives to refrigeration (on practical or aesthetic grounds) include the rural skills of drying (peas etc.) salting (meat and fish), and bottling (fruits and veg.)

3   *Scavenging Animals and Insects:* lots of possibilities here:
(a) Rabbits make very good protein as meat. Suitable varieties include English, Japanese, Himalayan, Belgium and Flemish Giant, Blue Imperial, Polish, Havanna Lop and New Zealand White. Hutches should be strongly built of wood and chicken wire or waterproofed mud, plaster or papier-mâché etc. Give rabbit 3 ft. x 2 ft. 6 in. floor space and get unit clear of ground-level. Keep well ventilated and out of strong sunlight. Bedding of sand, saw-dust, or dried leaves should be kept clean. Plenty of clean, fresh water. It is also possible to grow grass hydroponically (see 8) on a seven-day cycle!
(b) Giant Carp – could be used in ponds or tanks(?) to clean up organic pollution and to provide first-class food.
(c) Free Range Pigs – very thorough feeders on domestic food surplus and residues.
(d) Guinea Pigs – also good.
(e) Hens and Goats – value of goats questioned by other experts.
(f) House Flies – can be used to re-cycle chicken manure. Presumably they feed on the droppings and are eaten by hens and other small creatures.
(g) Microbes and algae – can be encouraged to produce a food cycle for herbivores such as rabbits (see 8f).
(i) Black Water Fly – used in Africa for animal and human protein source.
(i) Evolve your own insect farm to help in a food-chain. Attract them at night with lights (ultra-violet best) and trap with help of friendly spiders or nets, etc.

4 *Clothing Manufacture:* (a) Sheep's Wool; if you keep sheep, this would be perfect.
(b) Nettle Fibre.
(c) Fibrous material left over from leaf-protein masher (see 8d) could be woven and waterproofed with linseed oil.
(d) Flax – can be grown in temperate climates and needs only retting before removal of the fibre.

5 *Water Filter:* boxes or tubes filled with sand etc. Nylon/Terylene conical filters have been recommended for the efficient removal of most impurities. Biggest problem seems to be the heavy metals in urban rainwater, especially lead from petrol exhausts: —remedies include Reverse Osmosis (squeezing water through semi-permeable membranes) and filter beds of crushed glass.

6 *Food Consumption:* important to make best use of available diet.
(a) Eat little and often.
(b) Don't eat like a pig.
(c) Don't eat while worried or upset.
(d) Combine a little unfamiliar food with usual diet and increase gradually.
(e) If toothless; get good choppers.
(f) Eat nothing that will not rot, spoil or decay, but be sure to eat it before it does so.

7 *Food Preparation and Cooking:* (a) Wash or spray food *rapidly* with water to conserve the vitamins (soaking removes).
(b) Eat as many fruits and vegetables uncooked as possible. They provide cancer-protecting Catalase which is destroyed by cooking.
(c) Store fats and perishable food in cool, closed containers or fridge.
(d) Steam vegetables or drop in minimum of boiling water: cook rapidly with lid on.
(e) Scrub roots well (mineral content mainly in skin), rather than peeling, prepare all food just before cooking, and salads just before you eat.
(f) Cook any frozen food whilst still frozen.
(g) Keep all vegetable water to add to the food (gravy or soup etc.)

(h) Don't use soda with greens.

(i) Don't stir air into foods while cooking, or sieve or liquidise until cool.

(i) Don't overcook.

8 *Food Growing:* (a) Soya Beans are high protein vegetable.

(b) Sunflower seeds are reckoned to be almost as nutritious as soyas.

(c) Hydroponics – very simple method of soilless gardening; liquid nutrients can be made up from fertilizers or derived from processed sewage. Growth and nutritional value is reputed to be better than soil-grown produce.

(d) Leaf Protein extraction possible with mechanical (or hand?) pulping and heating machine to produce edible curd. (It has been found that fibrous, leafy crops which are normally fed to animals contain more protein than others more tender and popular with humans). Main problem seems to be in overcoming our prejudice for novel tastes. We need to get scientists collaborating creatively with inventive cooks.

(e) Research now being carried out on the amino acid (protein) balance of Haricot and Butter Beans.

(f) Single Cell Protein-microbial and algae foods; these can be grown in conjunction with grass roots (as host) to increase protein content to 40% for human consumption. Can also provide balanced diet for herbivores. In Japan, Chlorella algae is used for food and grown in polythene tubes which are strung across rooftops.

(g) Large Edible Fungi – be careful not to eat poisonous varieties. Expert knowledge needed for identification.

(h) Herbs – too many to list here. Useful for medicinal and important nutritional purposes.

(i) Biological Control of pests.

9 *Washing and Cleaning:* (a) Fog-Gun – atomises warm water and solvents with air under pressure. Compressed air on surface of skin *can be very dangerous* (can cause lethal bubbles of air in blood). But if set up correctly, this system can give 'baths' of up to an hour using only one pint of water which is by this time evaporated.

(b) Ultrasonic Washing Machine – normally a complicated device with numerous electronic parts (vibrates clothes under water at frequency higher than sound). Would it be possible to construct a fluidic version with no moving parts except a hand-powered pump? Suggested frequency 80 khz/sec at 50-150 watts. A real luxury, but an ecologically sound consumer product.

10 *Lavatory:* Graham Caine has a two-pint water squirter in his Eco-House design, to flush and to keep paper out of the system (combined flusher and bidet).

11 *Methane Plant:* the gas (similar to N. Sea gas) is the result of decomposing algae working on sewage and organic waste. In addition to gas for cooking, Carbon Dioxide can be used in the food growing section to enhance growth. Hydrogen Sulphide may also be present which may provide sulphur for organic insecticide solution. Methane may also be used in (slightly modified) petrol engines. Estimated 15 kW of power available from one acre of sunlit algae. In colder climates temperature may have to be kept to above 50° F or preferably up to 95°F.

12 *Telephone, T.V. and Lights.*

13 *Domestic Waste Tank:* this is really part of the sewage-to-methane process and the organic matter eventually provides liquid nutrient for the hydroponic process (see 8) or dry fertiliser for soil-grown plants.

14 *Sewage Tank:* as with the Organic Refuse Tank (13) this is an aerobic process like composting. A separate compost heap surrounding the tank may help to maintain the required temperature. Unlike the Methane Plant, which needs a sealed vessel to maintain anaerobic action and gas pressure, only a weighted compacting lid is strictly necessary. (This may be inadequate for reasons of hygiene).

15 *Heat Pump:* basically a fridge in reverse; transfers heat from large land-mass or water volume to a much smaller location thus raising temperature in that spot. Demands fairly extensive piping under surrounding terrain and may be ineffective in country. The inventor has patents on a system claimed to work in U.K. climate.

16 *Windmill Generator and Power Storage:* good field for the mechanically minded; ex Government or Car-surplus dynamo etc. with old batteries if available. Better bet from conservation of

metal standpoint is mechanical store of energy such as a weight on a winch which can be allowed to drop to turn the dynamo.

Similar principle used can be used with water (windmill) pumped from lower tank or pond to large upper tank; as it flows back it turns turbine and generator. Other alternatives include hydrolysis of water (electrical separation of hydrogen and oxygen) the stored gases can be re-united in a fuel cell to produce an electric potential.

SIMPLER WAYS AND HAPPINESS

To most industrially-conditioned individuals the ideas of self-sufficiency and eco-units may seem rather far-fetched, but it could well be that thousands, perhaps hundreds of thousands, of men and women, with their children, opting out of modern Western societies, could find real happiness and fulfilment in such simpler ways of living. Moreover, if man's greed and polluting activities should eventually bring about the destruction of civilisation, as we now know it, with widespread natural catastrophes caused by the thoughtless and irresponsible manipulation of the biosphere by human beings ignorant of ecological principles and practices, then very possibly the only people to survive the consequent breakdown of this technological age will be those who have taken refuge in self-sustaining eco-units and built up their own alternative methods of life. There is little doubt that many general benefits would accrue to urban dwellers if they would make even small efforts to resume contacts with nature and take advantage of applied ecological techniques in doing something for themselves, instead of always relying on being supported by centralised, artificial services. It is suggested that the following six advantages could be secured by any towns-person, living in an industrial area, if he or she would be agreeable to go just a little way towards some type of ecologic living pattern:

1. Development of more personal confidence.
2. Increase in adaptive abilities.
3. Capacity to resolve ambiguity and to cope with complexity.
4. Understanding of own ecological significance.
5. Increased innovative powers.
6. Movement towards a positive life style.

Why not think it over? Perhaps you might find that living in a practical ecologically based environment would develop your personality, change your behaviour, increase your skill in decision making, foster your creative side, remove many frustrations, and lead you to a truer and surer comprehension of the real world.

CHAPTER TWELVE

The Ecological Viewpoint

If anyone should ask: 'What is the most significant and out-standing fact of ecology, other than the distinctive concern that it expresses about the interrelationships of living organisms with the environments in which they exist?' a single answer would immediately spring to mind: 'Its broad and comprehensive view-point.' Ecology, especially in the applied field, is markedly different from nearly all other sciences, because it looks at affairs, not as might a narrow and rather restricted discipline, but as a far-reaching and all-embracing technique and system of active enquiry and methodical participation in the events that take place around us. The broad and comprehensive approach taught ensures that the various aspects and influences that shape and condition life are considered, evaluated and investigated, without prejudice or favouritism, and placed in their appropriate cate-gories. Nothing is neglected or omitted. Narrow specialisation cannot answer these complex questions. Hence the vital need for applied ecology to be flexible and fully comprehensive in all its divisions. No sections of life are too small or insignificant to be included in the purview of ecological investigation, whilst none are too big, because they are all interrelated and interconnected, in some manner or other.

NEW OUTLOOKS

When you take up the study of applied ecology, you will soon find that your outlook on life and world events is changing, per-haps slowly, but nevertheless inevitably. You will begin to view matters with what we may call an ecological eye; you will see the reality behind the appearance, and the truth behind the pretensions and the false fronts. In other words, you will com-mence to get attuned with nature and know what is actually happening all around you. Moreover, you will discover that using ecological principles and practical techniques to study and assess other organisms and situations may bring unexpected enlightenment and provide efficient and useful guidance in solving problems and overcoming difficulties.

Of course, ecology is a vast subject, with many ramifications, and naturally how you employ it and apply it in your own life and the lives of others will depend on the skill that you may acquire in deploying all the facts and methods that you have learned, or will learn in course of time. You can, if you wish, concentrate on particular sections of the science; or you can decide to utilise the general pattern of ecological thinking and practice over the whole field of your activities. This book is intended to serve as an introduction and guide to basic applied ecology. Consequently, it cannot do more than explain in clear and simple terms the scope of the science, and in addition set out working instructions for the initial steps that readers may wish to take in the direction of becoming amateur ecologists. Nevertheless, by using the information given and practising some of the suggested tests and observations, any ordinary person can acquire a sound general knowledge of the subject, with enough skills to apply ecological methods in his or her daily life.

THE ECOLOGICAL APPROACH

Over three centuries ago the English poet John Donne wrote: 'No man is an *Island*, entire of it self.'* These are significant words, faulty in simply one respect – they do not go far enough. For, in fact, it is not only men who are dependent upon their fellows. All living organisms, whether plants, animals, or human beings are similarly incapable of existing in complete isolation. Sentient life and capacity for motion do not lessen the need for food or raw materials which must be obtained, partly or wholly, from other creatures, or else from vegetation. Ultimately, too, it is only the activities of green plants in providing essential supplies of oxygen for respiration that enable life, as we know it, to continue on this planet. In addition to these fundamental relationships which ensure that they receive basic nourishment and air to breathe, organisms are affected directly or indirectly in numerous ways by the habits or behaviour of the different plants and animals existing around them. Predacition or aggres-

Devotions, John Donne (1571–1631).

sion can result in the extinction or diminution of populations, and there is usually greater or lesser competition for available food supplies.

On the other hand, certain advantages can frequently be gained from external contacts, such as concealment, provision of shelter, protection, vital materials, and various connected benefits. Animals produce their own effects upon neighbouring individuals and communities. Some of them eat or destroy competing species, even to the extent of altering an established balance of nature in particular cases. Many enter into reciprocal relationships with dissimilar types of organisms, so setting up forms of profitable co-existence; others burrow in the ground or trample the earth and thus influence local configuration and surface, as well as subterranean, features. Deposition of excreta by animals and birds aids in the fertilisation of land and assists in improving the texture of soils.

Higher plants, though possessing the ability to manufacture their own food by photosynthesis, are still obliged to rely upon animal respiration for at least part of the carbon dioxide necessary for this process. Supplies of the mineral salts that they draw up through their roots are maintained normally by the activities of fungi and bacteria present in the ground, which break down organic matter deposited by other living creatures or resulting from the decay of vegetable remains. Pollination or seed disposal may frequently depend upon the movement of animals, birds, and insects. All plant life, however peaceful it may appear to the eyes of the casual observer, is actually engaged in fierce competition and intense conflict, within its own society or with neighbouring communities and individuals, for such vital needs as light, water, nutrient salts, and space. While vegetation cannot indulge in violent physical fighting as animals and men do, yet wars amongst its components may be no less deadly. The main weapons of plants in their struggles are the overshading of rivals and the conquest and occupation of territory. In addition, some species (such as *Tagetes*) are capable of exuding chemicals which suppress effectively the germination of the seeds of competing types which may be lying close to them in the soil, or which can repel the attacks of ground pests.

It will therefore be apparent that the world in which we live is governed from day to day by a continual and challenging interplay of relationships between its constituent organisms. In this process of change and development all men, plants and animals exert numerous direct and indirect influences on one another and upon their various environments. Where well-defined communities exist, certain balances will be attained, conditioned not only by physical factors like light, temperature, humidity, and topography, but also by the complex associations formed amongst the contrasting life types. Such equilibria are often precarious and can be destroyed or altered quite rapidly by slight shifts of the influences involved. If the succeeding conditions should prove to be of adverse nature, then the results of upsetting a balance of life forces may well be disastrous or even catastrophic to the entire population of the area or localities in question. Consequently, a correct knowledge of these different interrelationships which can exist between organisms and their environments, and of the forces that bring them into being, affect their continuation, or terminate their periods of usefulness, is a matter of profound importance. For it is upon a proper understanding of the principles that underlie all this movement and flux that the health of the world's peoples and lands, and the future society of our planet, ultimately depend.

Fortunately during the past fifty years there has gradually grown up amongst many people a better appreciation generally of the need for a sound programme of global land health and the effective conservation and use of Earth's natural resources, both to preserve for posterity the limited assets available and to provide a sufficiency of food for the rapidly increasing world population. The foundations of this new outlook, however, go back as far as 1866, when Haeckel first introduced the word ecology as a definitive term for what was then a comparatively novel subject – the science of the study of organisms in relation to their environments. By seeking to explain the intricate and various bonds which arise between the different members of any community and to provide realistic understanding of societies as whole units or living complexes, practical ecology has provided mankind with an efficient means of mitigating harmful practices and adjusting present and future developments in the best interests of humanity.

The adoption of an ecological approach to development or conservation implies above all else that operations should be planned and managed as one co-ordinated whole. To achieve positive land health it is imperative that utilisation proceeds in accordance with the productive capacity of the ground. Normally this will depend upon what communities an area can support, which in turn hinges on factors of soil and climate. The status of local vegetation determines the fixing of solar energy in organic matter. Such fixed energy passes from plants to the animals feeding off them, and so right up the food chain until it is finally dispersed in respiration. It is therefore clear that the carrying capacity of land must be based, of necessity, upon the ability of its plant communities to fix energy. Apart from climate, soil and water are essential to the successful continuation and high output of this process. Hence the vital importance of conserving land to maintain good productivity, and of managing it in such a way that it should continue to yield profitable crops of economic value for an indefinite time in the future.

Application in practice of ecological principles has brought about the introduction of an ecological technology. Here we have working techniques which enable us to employ in field operations a thorough and detailed series of methods. These are designed entirely to secure the advantages of co-ordinated assessment and planning. Whether for the renovation of degraded lands or the opening up of new localities, these methods can provide safe and sure guidance for balanced and efficient development. Additionally, they may indicate with striking clarity the various pitfalls that must be avoided if satisfactory production is to be achieved and maintained. To carry out such methods the science of ecology draws upon other disciplines, for the 'ecological point of view' is, after all, nothing more than an attempt to work in harmony with nature. Solutions are sought which can help individuals and communities to live in the environments that force of circumstances compel them to exist in, or which have been developed by man's creative activity. The final aim is to secure profitable integration of the various factors that assist in the understanding of problems. It is often salutory to remember that man cannot fight nature directly; he has as it were to deceive her, to get her to nourish and sustain his own creations like inducing a foster-mother to suckle a foundling child. Then again, the production of food and materials, in the quantities that we need today to supply and support the human race, is by its very intensity and vastness, something that runs counter to the original scheme of life. There is still much truth in the words: 'in the sweat of thy face shalt thou eat bread . . .'* It is the main task of ecology to try to mitigate this ancient curse. So the importance of the ecological approach becomes plain and obvious and the part that it has to play in maintaining the health of our Earth and increasing its usefulness and productivity hardly requires any further emphasis.

By providing man with a scientific means of studying and dissecting the whole maze and tangle of interrelationships that bind organisms and their environments in countless series of fluctuating ecosystems, ecology has given humanity an asset of great value. But it would go without saying that if this key of knowledge and understanding was limited merely to the examination and classification of life forms and habitats its usefulness would be circumscribed severely. Happily, this is not the case. Ecology, as a science, is today an eminently practical discipline, constituting a tool that can be employed in everyday life to tackle all manner of problems in down-to-earth and straightforward terms.

MACHINES

It would be unrealistic if we should forget to discuss, before concluding this chapter, the subject of machines. Machinery of all types and forms exercises a profound influence on the lives of individuals and societies throughout the world. In addition, the emissions from machines, such as noise, poisonous gases, fumes, and vibrations, affect both biological organisms and their habitats in general adversely. Whilst modern technological groups could not exist in the manner that they do without machinery, it is no exaggeration to say that its employment and use have become uncontrolled in many places with disastrous results. As J. Huxley commented, man's greed, frequently expressed through his machines, has caused the despoliation of nature at an alarming rate. He went on to say: 'Wildlife is being exterminated; forests are being cut down, mountains gashed by hydroelectric projects, wildernesses plastered with mine shafts and tourists camps, fields and meadows stripped away for

*Genesis 3, v. 19.

Figure 28 Anthropomorphism in machines. In making motor cars, man has patterned their appearance on his own looks and features, thus virtually ascribing human characteristics to what is not human.

roads and airports.' Such actions, made possible because human beings have produced machinery to carry them out, are not planned with a view to benefiting people in general, but simply motivated by blind and stupid lust for profits and a hard and selfish cupidity.

Technological change, inevitable in view of man's position as a tool-maker, means that greater and more powerful machines, not only for performing physical tasks, but also for carrying ont intellectual exercises, will proliferate. Computers now undertake complicated calculations and store knowledge. As the process of development continues, human beings become slaves of the machines, inasmuch as their working lives may be spent in tending them and their domestic existences centered around them. In many modern industrial societies the new household gods are the television set and the motor car. The factor of aggression, inherent in all organisms, finds an excellent outlet through these contrivances, as they are manipulated by stronger individuals and populations or groups to secure advantages over the weaker sections of communities. Here we come across an interesting phenomenon: that of *anthropomorphosis* (transformation into human shape). Anthropomorphous machines are more the rule than the exception. In fabricating his machinery, man has patterned its appearance on his own features and looks. Thus we can observe that the fronts of motor cars, with their twin headlamps, frowning or cheerful radiators and hoods, and other appurtenances, resemble the human face. The aeroplane is modelled on the shapes of birds and insects. The hull of a ship is built like the body of a fish. Similar connections can be traced through the whole range of machines, some details or others of which invariably have anthropomorphic or zoomorphic associations. In ecological terms, it is apparent that unless man takes urgent steps to control his use of machinery, the ecosystems in which we live are going to suffer increased strains and stresses, which may eventually destroy them.

A WAY OF LIFE
Once you have adopted ecological patterns of thought, you will find that you have entered upon a new way of ife. Applied ecology cannot be classed as just another skill, such as typing, carpentry, engineering, medicine, politics, law, warfare, or dozens of other trades and professions. It is far too broad-based and comprehensive for placing in those categories. Since it transcends all those jobs and yet permeates through all walks of life, it becomes for individuals and communities a distinctive method of procedure or habit of doing things. Evaluating situations and problems in ecological style develops in the mind a way of viewing the world which is quite different from many conventional and prejudiced or narrow and rather limited outlooks. So when you take up ecological studies remember that you are embarking upon a new and exciting way of life. As time passes, you should find your enthusiasm grows. Did not the great Louis Pasteur (1822-1895) state that enthusiasm was vital to all scientific effort, which without this quality in its practitioners, would be little short of useless in practical terms?

FURTHER READING
Here are the names of some useful books and other literature that may be of value to readers interested in studying more about

ecology. In cases where they may not be available in local bookshops, copies might be borrowed from public libraries.

Books

Animal Ecology, S. C. Kendeigh, Prentice-Hall, New York.

Beginner's Guide to Hydroponics, J. Sholto Douglas, Pelham Books, London.

The Desert, A. S. Leopold, Time Inc. (Life Nature Library, New York.

Ecology, E. P. Odum, Holt Rinehart & Winston Inc., New York.

Ecology of Inland Waters and Estuaries, G. P. Reid, Reinhold Pub. Corpn., New York.

Exploring the Secrets of the Sea, W. J. Cromie, Prentic-Hall Inc., New York.

Food Resources Conventional and Novel, N. W. Pirie, Pelican.

The Forest, P. Farb, Time Inc. (Life Nature Library), New York.

Fundamentals of Limnology, F. Ruttner, University of Toronto Press, Toronto.

Human Ecology, J. A. Quinn, New York.

Introduction to Plant Ecology, M. Ashby, Macmillan & Co., London.

Last Whole Earth Catalogue, Unicorn Bookshop, 50 Gloucester Road, Brighton.

Management of Artificial Lakes and Ponds, G. W. Bennett, Reinhold Pub. Corpn., New York.

Man and the Land, L. D. Stamp, W. Collins & Co., London.

Man's Role in Changing the Face of the Earth, W. F. Thomas, University of Chicago Press, Chicago.

Natural Principles of Land Use, H. H. Graham, Oxford University Press London.

Plant Ecology, J. E. Weaver and F. E. Clements, McGraw-Hill Inc., New York.

The Poles, W. Ley, Time Inc. (Life Nature Library), New York.

Principles of General Ecology, A. M. Woodbury, Blakiston Inc., New York.

The Sea Around Us, R. Carson, Oxford University Press, London.

The Sea Shore, C. M. Yonge, W. Collins & Co., London.

The Study of Plant Communities, H. J. Oosting, W. H. Freeman Inc., San Francisco.

Survival Scrapbooks 1, 2, Unicorn Bookshop, 50 Gloucester Road, Brighton.
The Tropical Rain Forest, P. W. Richard, Cambridge University Press, London.
The Tropics, F. Bourlière and others, Knopf Inc. New York.

Journals
Alternative Technology, Impact of Science on Society, UNESCO, Paris, Quarterly, No. 4, Vol. XXIII, 1973.
Bulletin of the Ecological Society of America.
Ecological Monographs, Ecological Society of America.
The Ecologist, monthly, London.
Ecology, Ecological Society of America.
Journal of Animal Ecology, thrice-yearly, Blackwell Scientific Publications, Ltd., Oxford.
Journal of Applied Ecology, thrice-yearly,
Blackwell Scientific Publications Ltd., Oxford.
Journal of Ecology, British Ecological Society, thrice-yearly, Blackwell Scientic Publications, Oxford.
New Scientist, weekly, London.
Scientific American, monthly, New York.

Useful Associations
Henry Doubleday Research Association
20 Convent Lane, Bocking
Braintree, Essex.
(have kindly offered to send leaflet *Basic Food Guide* free to any reader who sends stamped addressed envelope. Also complete list of other publications.
Soil Association
Walnut Tree Manor
Haughley, Suffolk 1P143RS
The Rodale Press
Berkhamstead, Herts.
(publishes *Organic Gardening and Farming,* monthly.
Harold Bates
Pennyrowden
Blackawton
Totnes, Devon TQA 7ON.
(Two publications on methane, also car conversion kits).

Index